T0361765

Also by David L. Bahnsen

There's No Free Lunch: 250 Economic Truths

*The Case for Dividend Growth: Investing
in a Post-Crisis World*

*Crisis of Responsibility: Our Cultural Addiction
to Blame and How You Can Cure It*

FULL-TIME

WORK AND THE MEANING OF LIFE

DAVID L. BAHNSEN

Post Hill
PRESS

A POST HILL PRESS BOOK
ISBN: 979-8-89565-146-9

Full-Time:
Work and the Meaning of Life
© 2024 by Bahnsen Pub, LLC
All Rights Reserved
First Post Hill Press Hardcover Edition: February 2024

Cover art by Mina Widmer

Post Hill Press
New York • Nashville
posthillpress.com

Published in the United States of America
1 2 3 4 5 6 7 8 9 10

DEDICATION

This book is dedicated to the memory of my father, Dr. Gregory Lyle Bahnsen, who did more work in forty-seven years than most could hope to do in double that lifespan. Through his own indescribable and inspiring productivity, he taught me the *telos* found in work. He was the embodiment of diligence, focus, and calling fulfilled.

The visual memory I carry of finding him in his study, every single morning, working, is the best visual memory any father could leave his son. The joy he derived from studying, writing, preaching, and ministering as a scholar created this book.

He was an amazing father, friend, and person. He taught me more than I could ever capture in one book. As I have said many times since we lost him, if I have any good characteristics, I got them from him.

And that includes a love for work.

"And do not be conformed to this world, but be transformed by the renewing of your mind, that you may prove what the will of God is, that which is good and acceptable and perfect."

—*Romans 12:2 (NASB)*

TABLE OF CONTENTS

FOREWORD

In recent decades, books purporting to offer a distinctly Christian view of vocation, business, and work have rivaled their secular counterparts, ubiquitous on airport bookshelves. Christian titles are fewer numerically, but not proportionately. Quick-read tracts by Christian authors churn from the Christian presses, usually declaiming on the hazards of vocation and work to family and church life or limiting the objective of vocation and work to providing for one's family needs or financing Christian ministries. They are buttressed by pietistic Christian businessmen's conferences ("make lots of money so you can give it all away for your faith") and guilt-inducing church breakout sessions ("God made you rich so you can finance our latest capital building campaign"). No matter how diverse, almost all hold this in common: a shriveled, truncated, one-dimensional approach to vocation and work.

Not Bahnsen's book. To my knowledge, his is the first book in Christian history to address this all-important cluster of topics from the standpoint of creation. You'd think Christians, of all people, would begin where God begins in the Bible: at the beginning. Alas, almost all begin with cherry-picked, decontextualized Bible verses; broad, vague religious principles; or a Christian veneer decorating humanistic principles. It compounds their error that they tend to embrace an otherworldly pietism, floating in helium holiness high above the earth that God created man to cultivate for his glory, the world where diligence, creativity, thrift, productivity, savings, investment, delayed gratification, and wealth are bywords of a robust creational human life. Starting in the wrong place, they inevitably end up in the wrong place.

For too long, Christians have posited vocation and work as means to deeper, more "spiritual" ends like capitalizing churches, Christian schools, and mission projects. Or they perceive the chief aim of Christians' wage earning to be providing for one's family. Neither of these objectives are mistaken. Indeed, both are necessary. Where this thesis fails is in not seeing vocation and work as ends in themselves—as callings God placed man in the world to do for his glory. If anything, financing family, church, and Christian ministry is the glorious byproduct of a more basic calling: productively cultivating God's very good earth for his glory. That this sentiment sounds so odd, even unspiritual and "worldly," to modern Christian ears exhibits how deeply we've fallen from Biblical faith.

Unlike so many other treatments, Bahnsen's doesn't attempt to "integrate faith and work." This common integration project is part of the problem. The Bible's creational worldview doesn't integrate faith and work. It recognizes that work and vocation are part of what it means to be man and woman created in God's image. The faith itself grows partly out of just this stewardship calling given to humanity in Genesis 1. Work and vocation aren't cumbersome, post-fall add-ons to the world; God's good world was created precisely for man's work and vocation. This means that where there is no work and vocation, there can be no world.

This is a paradigm-shifting book. To adopt its thesis will lead over time to a series of extensive changes in one's worldview and life, toppling erroneous intellectual dominoes, and in the process altering one's Christian living across the board. It will produce a different—and better—kind of Christian.

David Bahnsen is one of my dearest friends, but don't assume my words are affectionate hyperbole. Read the book. Make your own objective assessment. I can promise you: you've never read anything like it, and that is as much a negative verdict on recent Christian thought as it is a commendation of David's thesis.

David Bahnsen has written a number of superb books, but if he'd never written another than this one, it would have been sufficient for a lifetime.

That's how good this book is. But don't take my word for it.

Read the book.

P. Andrew Sandlin
Founder and President,
Center for Cultural Leadership

INTRODUCTION

Work is not, primarily, a thing one does to live, but the thing one lives to do. It is, or it should be, the full expression of the worker's faculties, the medium in which he offers himself to God.

—Dorothy Sayers

There is no topic that animates me more than the subject of this book. I have wanted this book to be written for some time; though, I would have been perfectly happy if someone else had written it first. The perspective I intend to take in this book is not universally accepted, not mainstream, and may no longer even be acceptable to some. That said, I am convinced the argument I will make is right not only in its underlying message, but right in its points of emphasis, its hard edges, and even its potential to offend. *This book is going to argue that work is the meaning of life.*

I do not expect you to immediately agree with me on this. I only ask that you hear me out—allow me to make my argument in support of this thesis, address anticipated criticism, and provide deserved clarifications and caveats before you make your judgment.

My first book was called *Crisis of Responsibility: Our Cultural Addiction to Blame and How You Can Cure It.* Naïvely, I thought this book would generate controversy, poking people where they didn't want to be poked. In it I suggested that various institutional failures and policy errors (perceived or otherwise) of the day were not an open invitation to give up on one's own life. I pleaded from a sincere place of love and hope for people to cast off victimization and develop the individual resilience that could lead to a good life. I also argued that enough individuals developing personal resilience would build the collective resilience needed to improve policy, optimize our social framework, and move past an ideology of constant resentment.

Why did I believe this would be potentially offensive? Because I wasn't just suggesting that those on the left (accustomed to blaming race, class, or gender) needed to move past their grievances. No, I was maintaining that those on the right had to move past their blame of big government, big media, or big-whatever-else towards a more individually responsible and communally healthy end. The book did quite well for a first-time author, yet I never seemed to find people offended or bothered by the book.

What was my naïve error? I failed to see how many would agree in theory with what they virulently opposed in practice—those who love their own congressman but say they hate Congress, or those who say government spends too much money but have no specific budget item they are willing to cut. People tend to be very comfortable saying a life of blame casting is bad, just as long as they get to hold on to their own resentments and grievances. The book was macro-acceptable even as it was micro-ignored. Lesson learned.

I believe this book may upset people for reasons that are harder to ignore. Yes, there will be some who nod in agreement even as they ignore the real implications of what I am saying. But I believe there will be many more who are offended and bothered by the idea itself that work is the meaning of life. I sincerely hope they will hear me out.

On the other hand—and this gives me great hope—I believe there will be readers who have always believed work is good, but only to the extent that it leads to good things (a livelihood, family provision, tithes and offerings, a tax base). May they come away from this book seeing that work itself is inherently good, even when separated from utilitarian or pragmatic ends. I hold out hope that those who believe their career endeavors must create a certain *success* to enable them to enjoy a life of *significance* will instead appreciate their careers as inherently significant, vital, and meaningful.

My aspiration for this book is a dramatic reframing of the role work plays in our lives. My goal is to help the reader see that work is good, work is important, and work matters to God. I hope we can all see that God made humans to work, and that in work we function as an image-bearer of and cocreator with God.

This book's subject matter is not the only reason for my excitement in writing it. The categories the book covers are all passions of mine, and this is a rare opportunity to attempt to synthesize them into one coherent whole.

This book is deeply concerned with economic matters, and economic theory and practice are the focus of my professional life. My last book, *There's No Free Lunch: 250 Economic Truths*, was my attempt to rediscover the foundational truths underlying economics. One of the clearest economic principles is that production plays a powerful role in driving prosperity in a society. Pro-work ideology connects to economic life in a myriad of ways.

This book is also deeply theological. I am not a theologian; I am not ordained. I am, however, insistent on rooting all applied thought in a theological foundation. One's ultimate truth claims indicate who their God is, and my God is the triune God of the Bible. I am not alone in grounding economic and cultural applications in a theological foundation. And I would say that *all people* have theological and philosophical commitments that serve to formulate their theory and practice of a given discipline or subject. I want this book to be explicitly theological, i.e., studiously aligned with the revelation of Scripture.

This book is also explicitly ontological. I do not limit my arguments about work to the economic and theological; I work to provide readers with an introspective benefit for their own lives. It is incumbent on me to make the existential case for work being the meaning of life. I have significant things to say about despair, isolation, and hopelessness, and where work fits into a holistic subject on dignity, purpose, and hope.

This book aims to be practical. I am engaged in the business of private wealth management and have a close-up view of the world of financial services. How one integrates their beliefs and practices around work with fiscal reality is of paramount importance. In fact, I will argue that one of the greatest problems with so many books in the Christian marketplace on this subject is not so much what is said but rather what is ignored: money. I will not make an abstract argument for work, connecting it only to unobjectionable things like art and service, all while ignoring financial betterment and personal aspiration. Instead, I will seek to dismantle the unspoken attitude Americans are programmed (or marketed to) to take towards work—namely, that the purpose of work is to not have to do it anymore.

If you read this book and find it economically, theologically, ontologically, and practically useful, I will have succeeded. I believe the harmonization of all these components is the real task at hand.

The default view of secular culture and the church has been that our identities are not tied to what we do. Our value as humans, we are told, is unconnected to any aspect of what we offer society vocationally, professionally, or productively. Our identity and value exist in some ethereal realm, separate from physical and metaphysical reality.

This is, of course, utter nonsense. We don't hesitate to define our heroes by what they have done, and for good reason. The idea that a person can be metaphysically separated from what they do and have done is fantastical.

We certainly know that our standing before God is not based on our own work and activity (Protestants call this the doctrine of justification). Indeed, the redemptive work of Christ is divorced from our own merit, and I acknowledge that freely, without qualification.

We graciously don't often define a person by their lowest moments and their worst actions, but rather maintain a healthy regard for redemption and recovery. It is an endearing part of the American ethos—that we love a good redemption story. I am a sucker for one because I am one, as are all of us. So, I am not suggesting that bad actions define us, or that every part of our lives should be boiled down to the things we do.

When I argue that our value and identity in a human and practical dimension is derived from those things we do, I am not speaking of our eternal destiny. I am speaking of the contributions we make on earth. What one has to offer in skill, innovation, resilience, exertion, sacrifice, and productivity is not magically abstracted from their personhood—it is a key component of it.

And I am almost uncomfortable speaking about this because it risks being patronizing to an audience that *intuitively knows it is true.*

———————————

I think we are all familiar with the clichéd Hollywood setup of a man "married to his career" who over the course of the movie slowly realizes that he is missing out on the "important" things in life and eventually picks an alternative (a romance, his kids, more frequent walks through a garden, mentoring a troubled high school youth) over the "evils" of careerism and personal ambition. Listen, I want all these hard-charging guys to find themselves, revisit the demons of their youth, play soccer with their kids, and ride tandem bikes with their wife on the beach, just as much as the next man. What I find troubling is that this is often done as a (false) contrast with a high view of work.

My wife and I have watched the holiday classic *The Family Man* every single Christmas that we have been married. The lead character, played by Nicolas Cage, is a bachelor investment banker riding high on Wall Street. He is extravagant, self-centered, and shallow, and lacks any meaningful personal relationships. On Christmas Eve, he is visited by an angel of sorts and wakes up the next morning with a wife and kids in suburban New Jersey (his wife being the girlfriend of his youth who "got away"). Now look, the eponymous man is not a sympathetic character in real life, but he becomes a soft, sympathetic character in his imaginary life. Any decent person likes suburban "New Jersey Jack" more than "Park Avenue Jack." The scenes with his wife and kids are adorable. And as a family man myself who considers the family unit the primary building block of society—the pre-political unit God Himself ordained in the Garden of Eden—far be it from me to praise career at the expense of family. I do not.

But the opposite stereotypical contrast is not valid, either. "Career ambition" does not automatically entail "low view of family," nor does high value of family compel a low view of career. Paying serious attention to one's professional responsibilities does not translate to a low regard for personal character and virtue. But it's a false dichotomy that appears all over the place in pop culture: that serious ambition is the enemy of one's personal actualization, or well-being, or love for family.

The entire matter gets significantly worse when one moves from pop culture's misrepresentations of work to the church's almost explicit condemnation of careerism. Consider how sermons against careerism outnumber sermons against actually prevalent cultural sins by a wide margin. Lazy people far outnumber workaholics in pastors' congregations, but they nevertheless preach to the latter with all the urgency they can muster. I have heard more pastors than I can count say that "our value is not tied to what we have to offer." If all they meant was that the work of Christ on the cross was not tied to our contributions, great! But a creational theology about work (and wealth) is largely absent in today's church, replaced by safe, facile decrial of the "idolatry" of work. A latent dualism that pits the Kingdom of God against our productive endeavors on earth prevails.

Fortunately, there is a movement afoot to try and reconcile concerns about work with the clear tradition and teaching around work embedded in Christian theology. As I will dig into later in the book, there are signs of improvement in positive attitudes toward work. Overall, however, the work is incomplete. My task in this book is not to critique those who have made the case for a high view of work in the Christian life. Rather, it is to attempt to complete the work.

I have my own "greatest hits" list of books written by Christian scholars in defense of work, and I am beyond grateful for their contributions. Years ago, Tim Keller's *Every Good Endeavor* opened my eyes to the increased prevalence of a more thoroughly Christian view of work. Keller makes a theological case for work as a pre-sin reality of human existence and ties the practical (work as necessity for support) to the existential (work as a necessary component of our inner meaning and usefulness). Keller's assertions, along with those of several others I cite in this book, are sober-minded, substantial, and deeply appreciated by this author. My purpose is to expand upon these principles and develop a comprehensive case for work that incorporates economic, professional, anthropological, and financial elements. I want this expression to come without a presupposition of regret, doubt, hesitation, or apology. I want to make an emphatic embrace of work and ambition the name of the game, and I want to do this by grounding it in a true understanding of the human person and what God created us to do.

We don't pretend that Steve Jobs and the twenty-six-year-old playing video games all day in his mother's basement contributed the same thing to society—because they didn't. Everyone knows one outdid the other. Notice what I *didn't* say, though. I did not say that Steve Jobs's *soul* is more valuable than that of the twenty-six-year-old video game junkie. The inherent dignity of every human being was established at creation. At a functional level, however, there are concrete reasons to identify certain people as producing and achieving at a higher level. Let's not pretend that we cannot understand that Steve Jobs accomplished more for society than the twenty-six-year-old.

I am here to say that some football players are better than other players, some artists are better than other artists, and some achievements in the marketplace have a greater impact than others. And let's be honest: you believe that, too, even if it is uncomfortable to acknowledge. I also am here to say that some people work hard because they actually do believe that some of their value is tied to what they have to offer.

What we do is, of course, not limited to our vocations. Some people's greatest contribution may be the advice they give a friend, the encouragement they offer to a family member, the anonymous and invisible sacrifice they exerted at a given time, or any number of lower-profile moments of service, virtue, and heroism. I am not making the case that fame and prestige should define a person. I am, however, stating that a person's work and activities are clearly a part of their identity. And I believe that this should be celebrated, and maybe, just maybe, leaned into.

This book is not only for professionals, financiers, and Wall Street types, even though my own vocational calling concerns financial markets. Nor is it only for those whose work makes them well-known, elite, or simply wealthy. The topic of this book is relevant to them, but I will have missed the mark if the book's only takeaway is that high-paid careerists should feel better about what they do.

In fact, this book's conclusions do not change based on the income and status of a particular reader. The theological, economic, and practical message is universal. I am arguing for a call to productivity for all mankind, all who are made *imago dei*, with dignity and purpose. Readers' socioeconomic circumstances are irrelevant to the book's underlying message—

that God values what you do, and he does not value it merely because of some good that can come from it. God sees inherent goodness in all productive endeavors because God was and is their ultimate creator.

I will close this introduction with my promised caveats.

I do not write this book without my own biases. I am a dedicated worker and have been my entire adult life. I start work very early in the morning and think about my professional responsibilities around the clock. I would like to think I am a devoted husband and father, but I have sometimes struggled to succeed in all three roles (worker, husband, father). I am unapologetically ambitious and that can cause the telos—the ultimate aim—of my work to be missed or misunderstood.

I have what some like to call a "Type A" personality, and when I take the tests for any personality framework (Enneagram, Myers-Briggs, DISC, CliftonStrengths, etc.) they all indicate that mine is not the most popular or touchy-feely of personality types. Each of these tests is geared toward identifying one's general personality and propensity. They then elucidate ways people's differences can be used as strengths, create communication challenges, or be taken to excess. It's easy to list the potential downsides of a Type A way of being—we're an easy target, it seems. With that in mind, I can safely say that some will interpret this book as a self-serving defense of my own potential character flaws. Nothing could be further from the truth.

I will do my best throughout the book to affirm what so many skeptics of my thesis will want me to affirm: I believe that any false idol is bad. I am not writing a book in defense of idolizing work, career, ambition, or professional reputation. But I believe that more than one thing can be a counterfeit god in our age, and we seem to have become highly selective in which ones we target. Our children, our marriages, our churches, our communities, our friendships—all these relationships are good and vital, and all are susceptible to being prioritized unwisely. I do not believe that the best precaution against idolizing any of the above is to worry against being *too good* a spouse (or parent, or friend, or community member). It is possible both to be a great spouse by loving your partner wholeheartedly *and* not to rely on them for that which only God can provide.

While it would be unfathomable to speak of diluting our enthusiasm for any of these relationships, only work, vocation, activity, and ambition are held up as things that require temperance or reduction in effort for fear of excess (that, candidly, is much less prevalent than we tend to think). Yes, some in our society doubtless use their careers as an escape from or coping mechanism for a forsaken spirit. But we can have a vibrant relationship to our work and love it wholeheartedly without letting it take over our lives. I believe our work ought to be a gift that flows from our spirit, a vehicle for creating shalom and not a substitute for a real shalom. And, as I'll lay out in this book, the far greater risk in our society is the treatment of vocational responsibility as a chore and a bore.

I understand full well what criticisms will be leveled against me. I will be accused of materialism, of a low view of family, and of not appreciating the gravity of the problem of people trying to earn self-worth.

The opposite is true for each of those. I believe those who stand in the way of a robust view of work are the real materialists, opting to see work as merely transactional and utilitarian, ignoring the great *immaterial* benefits that it offers.

My view of family (as well as church, community, civil society, etc.) is not secondary to my views on the marketplace but rather in line with a holistic Kingdom theology that places all under the Lordship of Christ. As the great Abraham Kuyper said, "There is not a square inch in the whole domain of our human existence over which Christ, who is Sovereign over all, does not cry, 'Mine!'"

I confess to being an imperfect worker, husband, and father, but I do not believe that my imperfections in one are caused by excessive focus on another. Pitting one element of God's Kingdom against another is pitiful theology, and I ask you to take my allegiance to family and my view of work as part of the same theological message.

Finally, I promise you that I am aware of the reality of "unhealthy striving," that some people work one-hundred-plus hours per week out of vanity, escapism, and egotism. I believe that we have a better message for them than "work less," "do worse," and "your activities don't matter" (all of which are likely terrible advice). Rather, I believe a message of tethering their endeavors to the created order, connecting their ambitions to the cause of human flourishing, is what's called for. Even when someone truly is a workaholic (they often aren't), the prescription is almost always wrong. Far from trying to ignore those diagnoses, I am trying to prescribe a true cure.

At the same time, we must stop enabling a far greater epidemic in society—not of overachieving, but of hating achievement. Not of workaholism, but of "no-aholism"—no passion, no purpose, and no plan. I am writing this book because this gap is where a true, animating doctrine of work is most needed.

My passion for this subject is not self-serving and should never lead to a forfeiture of civility and sincerity. But there are some hard truths that have to be told in order to craft a narrative about work that is cogent economically, deeply rooted theologically, and properly ordered ontologically. If I offend, forgive me; if I fail to convey my conviction, do not. The stakes are higher here than any issue I could choose to write about. For as my favorite workaholic of the sixteenth century said:

> *The Lord bids each one of us in all of life's actions to look to His calling.... [E]ach individual has his own kind of living assigned to him by the Lord as a sort of sentry post so that he may not heedlessly wander throughout life.... The Lord's calling is...the beginning and foundation of well-doing.... [N]o task will be so sordid and base, provided you obey your calling in it, that will not shine and be reckoned very precious in God's sight.*

> —*John Calvin*

A CRISIS OF DESPAIR

DIGNITY AND EARNED SUCCESS

DOOR-TO-DOOR LAWNMOWING

FIRST JOB - AGE 12

If you don't connect yourself to your family and to the world in some fashion, through your job or whatever it is you do, you feel like you're disappearing, you feel like you're fading away, you know? I think that feeling, wherever it appears...it's an enormous source of pain; the struggle to make yourself felt and visible. To have some impact, and to create meaning for yourself, and for the people you come in touch with.

—*Bruce Springsteen*

In this time of severe political tribalization and cultural disunity, there may be only one belief that is generally accepted on both sides of the political and cultural divide: *many people are alienated, unhappy, and estranged from traditional sources of contentment.* I cannot imagine a sociologist, psychologist, psychiatrist, educator, pastor, or pundit who would disagree. There is room to debate the reasons underlying this discontent and its possible remedies, but it's clear that social cohesion has deteriorated, and with it, individual happiness.

Arthur Brooks enumerates the four elements that contribute to happiness: *faith, family, friends, and work*. I am firmly convinced that these are the four ingredients that make up the recipe for a content and fulfilling adult life. A quick review of the current state of our alienation and unhappiness shows a loss in all four areas.

An Unhappy Picture of Our Loneliness and Isolation

There is plenty of statistical support for the contention that people are unhappy. Levels of self-declared depression and clinically diagnosed depressive symptoms have skyrocketed in recent years, a trend that was underway well before the COVID-19 pandemic.[1] Depression levels have worsened further since the onset of the pandemic,[2] a development I will argue is heavily correlated to the decline in the workforce.

I wish I were merely talking about more adults confessing to being sad, but we are seeing an increase in depressed dispositions leading to an increase in behavior of desperation. The overall suicide rate increased a shocking 30 percent in the first twenty years of this new century.[3] Roughly 5 percent of American adults have reported serious thoughts of suicide.[4]

We know that alcohol and drug abuse has skyrocketed, and, in fact, deaths from alcohol abuse have risen precipitously, even for those over the age of sixty-five.[5] Nearly one million people

---

1   American Journal of Preventive Medicine, Volume 63, Issue 5, November 2022.

2   Boston University School of Public Health, "Persistent depressive symptoms during COVID-19: A national, population-representative, longitudinal study of U.S. adults," October 4, 2021.

3   Centers for Disease Control and Prevention, "Suicide Mortality in the United States," NCHS Data Brief No. 433, March 2022.

4   Mental Health America, "2022: The State of Mental Health in America," p. 22.

5   Dr. Ellen Kramarow, "Alcohol-Induced Deaths in Adults Aged 65 and Over," National Center for Health Statistics, November 2022.

have died from drug overdoses in America since the year 2000, with a 30 percent increase in the number annually in recent years, and a 256 percent increase over that twenty-year period.[6] The escalation in the rate of growth of opioid deaths began just after the 2008 financial crisis. Separate from those who tragically die from drug- and alcohol-related causes, a stunning fifteen million Americans regularly abuse alcohol, 61.7 percent of whom are men.[7] The tragedy of lives consumed by drug and alcohol abuse is worsened only by deaths rooted in drug and alcohol abuse.

The use of antidepressants has doubled over the last twenty years, with a 35 percent increase in the last six years alone.[8] It is estimated that thirty-seven million American adults regularly take an antidepressant medication[9] (albeit at varying degrees of severity and dosage). We are talking about 15–20 percent of American adults needing medication for problems related to depression and anxiety.

Skyrocketing rates of suicide, depression, fatalities, drug abuse, and alcoholism are extreme examples stemming from a greater crisis of isolation. Over the last twenty years, the average time a person spends alone each day has grown from 285 minutes to 333 minutes, equivalent to over twelve additional days per year spent alone.[10] Time spent with friends has decreased by 37 percent in less than a decade.[11] Social isolation is not the same

---

6   Drug Overdose Death Rates, National Center for Drug Abuse Statistics, July 2022.

7   National Institute on Alcohol Abuse and Alcoholism, March 2022.

8   Centers for Disease Control and Prevention, NCHS Data Brief No. 377, September 2020.

9   "Health, Pharma, & Medtech: State of Health," Statista, April 2020.

10   Viji Kannan and Peter Veazie, "U.S. Trends in Social Isolation," Science Direct, p. 4.

11   Bureau of Labor Statistics, "American Time Use Survey: 2021 Results," June 23, 2022.

as being introverted (take it from this introvert). The increase in isolation is creating an inner loneliness, and that loneliness has become the primary social ailment of our day. These behaviors speak to a culture in despair.

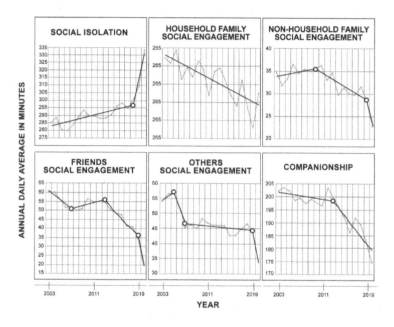

Science Direct, *"U.S. Trends in Social Isolation,"* Dr. Viji Kannan, Peter Veazie, p. 4

God-Sized Hole

First, I acknowledge that the specifics of where work and purpose fit into this must be understood in the context of greater spiritual alienation playing out in concert with secularization. To address the challenges that an inadequate view of work present, we must first understand that we face the possibility of misunderstanding the purpose of our existence. We'll spend more time on this in chapter 3, but as we examine this crisis of deep loneliness, we must acknowledge the transcendent truths that surround our own purpose and activity (and that our dislocation from them mirrors and exacerbates the isolation and despair I describe above).

We did not wake up one day despondent merely because we were becoming oblivious to the pleasures of using our minds and hands in daily labor. A common rejection of the truths that define reality has made a comfortable relationship with that reality impossible, and a secularized humanism that rejects God, creation, and the gospel message of redemption has done unspeakable damage to the pursuit of happiness. Many books have been written and many more surely will be about the psychological, spiritual, and intellectual deficits created in the human soul by rejecting transcendent truth. Modernism, post-modernism, and skepticism have done a lot of things, but not one of them is to establish a more contented and joyful society.

Delayed Family Values

A decline of faith has not occurred in a vacuum. Not coincidentally, a declining embrace of Christianity has corresponded with a decline of the family unit in modern society. Increased divorce rates, elevated numbers of kids growing up without both a loving mother and father in the home, and extended singleness have all taken a toll on the institution of family that has long been the building block of civilization.

Of course, one way to keep the divorce rate from going higher is to lower the marriage rate itself. We see the same number of new marriages per year now that we did in 1950, despite the fact that the population has more than doubled since then. The percentage of marriages that end in divorce has more than doubled over the last seventy years. Just over fifty years ago, 86 percent of children were raised with both a mom and dad in the home; the number is now 70 percent.[12] The percentage of homes where a child is living without a father present has doubled in that time period. The average age of a first marriage for men is now 30.1, and for women it is 28.2. That is a full eight more years of singleness than a generation ago (I realize some see this as a positive; I do not).

The Lost Art of Friendship

It turns out the negative effects of declining faith and deteriorating families extend into other relationships, as well. Twenty-two percent of Americans say it has been five years since they last made a new friend, and only 16 percent of Americans say they first go to a friend when they have a personal problem.[13] In 1990, 3 percent of Americans said they had "no close friends," whereas a stunning 12 percent say so now.[14] A quadrupling in thirty years of those who say they have no close friends is a national tragedy, but so is the data around the average number of professed close friends. Forty-seven percent of Americans said they had six or more close friends in 1990; only 25 percent say as much now.[15]

Three out of Four

Even those who reject faith in the real God of the Bible acknowledge some vague form of spirituality and transcendence as significant for psychological health. While the traditional family is

---

12   Census Bureau, "Current Population Survey," 2020.
13   Survey Center on American Life, "American Perspectives Survey," May 2021.
14   Gallup Organization, "Gallup News Service Poll: January 1990, Wave 2," Roper Center for Public Opinion Research, 1990, https://doi.org/10.25940/ROPER-31088676.
15   Ibid.

less highly regarded in today's secular environment, marriage and parenthood are still common, and companionship and community ties are still celebrated as a vital part of a life replete with belonging and purpose.

Whether it be the church or a secular outlet, some concept of faith, family, and friends is acknowledged as a positive counter to hyper-alienation and loneliness.

This is the value in the construction offered by Arthur Brooks regarding the basic recipe for happiness: *faith, family, friends, and work*. Where all these components are present in civil society, regardless of socioeconomic strata, greater happiness exists.

Charles Murray made the case in his masterful book *Coming Apart: The State of White America (1960-2010)* that the deterioration of all four of these components was central to the decline in American happiness.

> *When Americans used to brag about "the American way of life"—a phrase still in common use in 1960— they were talking about a civic culture that swept an extremely large proportion of Americans of all classes into its embrace. It was a culture encompassing shared experiences of daily life and shared assumptions about central American values involving marriage, honesty, hard work and religiosity.*[16]

The absence of any one of these four elements adds to the burden of the human condition, and the absence of all four of them presents a nearly unbearable state.

---

16   Charles Murray, "The New American Divide," *Wall Street Journal*, January 21, 2012.

Getting Down to Business

Faith, family, friends, and work all play a role in our happiness (or *un*happiness), yet only one is systemically blamed as a *source* of unhappiness. Even those who define the first three ingredients differently than I do acknowledge that they play a pivotal role in *some* way. Work, and work alone, is ignored or even regarded with hostility as a remedy to the isolation of our day. Work is routinely scapegoated as the problem (stress, burden of achievement, busyness) when, in fact, the purpose, activity, and usefulness it reinforces may be the best prescriptive remedy against the insidious alienation we face today.

Life's Lessons

It was my personal experience that first persuaded me that happiness was integrally connected to work; research and observation later convinced me that my experience was not unique, and that universal principles and realities existed that were being societally ignored at our own peril. If I were offering only a biographical anecdote, then I might be guilty of projection in making the case for work as a surmounting of life's challenges and burdens. Discard my experience as unique to my life if you wish, but please consider the deeper principles I appeal to as you evaluate this issue. I believe I am quite literally arguing for the happiness of humanity.

My father passed away at the age of forty-seven, shortly after I turned twenty-one, and I was devastated. My mother had been gone from our family for six years by then, and I essentially found myself without my hero and best friend, and without the family unit and structure that most people would rely on in such a traumatic experience. I had friends. I had brothers. Many people have been through worse. But at the heart of that loss was not merely the trauma of Dad's death—though it was surely that—but the "fork in the road" moment it produced. I had only known life with my dad, under his roof, in relationship with him. Now it was time to start life without yet an identity, a direction, or an aim. It was a daunting pivot point, to say the least.

As I get closer to age fifty, the beneficiary of a rewarding career and work life, I can barely imagine what those years would have been without work. The therapeutic reality of work—purpose and calling—in a prolonged moment of identity crisis and existential questioning was a gift from God. I do not mean that it was merely a diversion (though I will not join the chorus, either, of those who insist that "diversions" are always unhealthy— they have their place, too). Rather, I mean that I found in my work a substantive and healthy channel for purposeful activity. It provided me the purpose a young man dealing with a loss would need, and through time even became something I could connect to my own father and his life and work: why he did what he did; why I did what I did; what he wanted for his life; what I wanted for my life.

Arthur Brooks has codified the term "earned success" to capture the reason behind the psychological lift that productive work creates. The inner feeling of not just receiving something, but earning it, meaningfully forms the basis for self-worth and deserved recognition. The concept transcends time diversion and becomes a source of purpose. Importantly, it does this through the service of others, not the vanity of only serving oneself. This basic market reality is at the heart of the concept of earned success—we become valuable in the marketplace, and achieve this inner satisfaction, only when we are valuable to others through our service and work.

The specifics of my life experience are not material to the case I am making, which I believe to be universal. I am grateful that I am speaking from experience, but even if I were not, it is incontrovertibly true that earned success is a vital antidote to boredom, trauma, alienation, and depression. Achievement, productivity, and other forms of human activity that reflect our unique talents and passions *are the prescription.*

A Healthy Coping Mechanism

You often hear the expression "medicating through achievement," a snide expression of the belief that people may be dealing with their fears and insecurities by working too hard or using professional achievements as a substitute for a balanced and satisfying life. I have to wonder if thirty-seven million Americans quite literally medicating away anxieties and depressions renders that expression a poor choice of words. The state of society cries out *for* "medicating through achievement," rather than an increased supply of pharmaceuticals.

I am not suggesting that those with significant traumas ought to ignore coping and processing by burying themselves in their work. What I am suggesting is that any treatment for trauma that does not enable a person to marry their passion and their skills by pursuing achievement has failed. Work plays a role in treatment, and it is a necessary part of the outcome. We deal with our traumas so we can have happy lives, and we cannot have happy lives if we are not working, producing, and achieving. It is what God made us to do, each in our own unique and particular context.

We talk about loneliness as if it were simply the lack of a friend or a spouse, when I believe it should be wholly understood as the *lack of a purpose.* We desperately need friends and spouses to enjoy the vital social and relational dimensions of who we are and who we were created to be, but friends and spouses do not and cannot give us purpose.

Purpose is more than just "something to do with one's time," i.e., the opposite of idleness. It stands to reason that purpose counters idleness, but I am proposing that it does more than that. Purpose reverses a life where things are done *for us*, to a life where we do things *for others*. It facilitates a life not contingent on the approval of others, but rather, within our own agency. With purpose, the need is not to receive honor or respect, but to be honorable and respectable.[17] It addresses the issues not only of our *time*, but also of our *character*, by requiring service and sacrifice. It has an inner and outer focus—our internal hopes and dreams, and the external way in which they are achieved.

I found myself in a vulnerable stage of life because of loss, and my work could not bring back that which I had lost. Nothing can replace what we sometimes lose, but there are healthy ways in which we can overcome and move past such traumatic events. In my case, the loss of my dad was actually coupled with a tremendous insecurity about who I was, who I wanted to be, and what my purpose in life really was. My dad was my source of strength and inspiration in so many ways, but when he was no longer there, it accelerated my need for that inner discovery. The existential fears I had linked to the trauma of loss and sadness were healthily rectified over the years through work, earned success, and the productive endeavors that God made me for.

The Benefit of Purpose to Society

I am keenly aware that each person's journey will look different, and that the exact path I had is not the same each person will have. The universal principles of which I speak move us past the details of a certain trauma, challenge, or struggle, and address

---

17 David French, "Men Need Purpose More Than 'Respect,'" *New York Times*, February 12, 2023, https://www.nytimes.com/2023/02/12/opinion/men-purpose-respect.html.

the broadly human reality that *human beings crave a purpose.* This is true whether it is useful in a specific therapeutic context or not.

A recasting of purpose as a fundamental driver of work will do more for the social inequalities of various professional choices than economic interventions by the state. A society that rediscovers and reappreciates *purpose* in work and the concept of *service* in finding existential benefit no longer has to presuppose a hierarchy that elevates certain white-collar professions above blue-collar professions. Market forces may price the work of a lawyer or professor differently than that of a waitress or plumber in a monetary sense (dependent on subjective values embedded in supply and demand), and certain professions may require greater use of the mind than others and some greater use of the hands than others. But income, skill, intellect, and education are all disintermediated when it comes to the appreciation of *purpose*. A truck driver and a bond trader are on an even playing field in that important category. The way that we formulate our own hierarchies of one's importance should never have become based on income level or social strata, yet the surest way to reverse this unhealthy trend is to reframe our understanding of work as a productive act of purposeful service, not merely an act of economic climbing.

Our cultural presentation, our basic vocabulary, and our underlying intents and objectives must all reinforce work as a fundamental part of an optimal social order. All of society benefits from more people being engaged in productive activities, and all of society, therefore, has a moral obligation to say so. The habit of productive and fulfilled people speaking approvingly of people being unproductive (and therefore unfulfilled) is an outrageous form of hypocrisy.

This reframing also helps us to reject a dehumanizing attitude toward accountability and responsibility, without which people are robbed of their dignity and deprived of a pursuit of purpose fundamental to the achievement of a fulfilling life. The progressive world has no business implying that a workless life is an acceptable one, and it is even more shameful for the church to imply the same.

The declining social standards of the most unhappy and alienated parts of modern society create a negative feedback loop, further pushing down the view of work. We refuse to see the tremendous dignity engendered by discovering and implementing a solution, problem-solving, collaborating with coworkers, and meeting goals in a commercial context with common objectives. Consequently, antisocial activities have metastasized— obsessive video game playing, chronic drug and alcohol use, financial dependence on others, sexual irresponsibility, and on and on. Each step in the wrong direction makes one less productive, less employable, and less capable of partaking in the process of earned success. Each step in the right direction builds on itself in the opposite way: one's activities serve the needs of others, even as one's own needs can be met through compensation for one's labors. Behind one door is the satisfaction that comes from serving others and making one's own way; behind the other door is a constant reminder of one's own inadequacy, failure, and isolation.

The tone and tenor we take in discussing work today reeks of people who, themselves, have achieved "earned success"—i.e., possess some combination of faith, family, friends, and work— and yet seem unable or unwilling to share the formula with others. Worse, they seem willing to share the three noncontroversial parts but not the "secret sauce" that is perhaps the greatest factor in achieving this aim. So many successful, well-adjusted people wake up each day with purpose and contentment because they will be going to a job in which they are valuable, and yet publicly take a stance on work that is contradictory to their own life's circumstances.

Rounding Third for Home

Our society does not need to see this alienation epidemic grow any further. It needs a holistic reevaluation of work, rooted in the celebration of achievement and productivity. The work we celebrate should not be linked to social strata. Our aim must be celebration of lawyer and janitor alike, of those using their minds and those using their hands. Some jobs are stepping stones, some are dream jobs, and some are somewhere in between.

By embracing the "earned success" that comes out of marrying one's passions to one's skills, we can leave behind a culture of isolation, depression, and perpetual grievance. Instead, we are invited into a world of service, where our efforts serve others through the production of goods and services that meet the needs of humanity.

In so doing, the biggest winner is ourselves.

THE CURRENT
PANDEMIC

A SHRINKING WORKFORCE
STIFLES ECONOMIC GROWTH

MALL FOOD COURT SMOOTHIE SAMPLE HANDOUT

Come, labor on.
Who dares stand idle on the harvest plain
while all around us waves the golden grain?
And to each servant does the Master say,
"Go work today."

—*Jane L. Borthwick*

The last chapter addressed how high levels of purposelessness contribute to the growth in despair that plagues society. That despair is evident in the rise of isolation, substance abuse, loneliness, and more. The psychological and emotional toll taken on the soul of society has been severe. Work is the antidote to this malady and yet it is often presented as part of the problem.

This chapter takes a different approach to the same topic, but one that is more obvious. "*The solution to a declining labor force is an increasing labor force*" is a more self-evident argument than "*A crisis of despair can be met with the antidote of work.*" I believe both, but the first statement rings true more intuitively than the second. That said, both describe an enormous risk to us all.

But yes, there is a need to first make the case that the workforce is shrinking, and then to make the case that this is an economic disaster. Once this is established, unpacking the solution is easy. Consider this chapter a historical case as much as an economic one.

Our study has to begin with a basic empirical analysis of the labor participation force. Simply put, the labor force is the number of those with a job plus those looking for a job. The labor participation rate is the proportion of the total labor force to the total working-age population. So, the labor participation rate is those age sixteen or over with a job or looking for a job, divided by the total population of those age sixteen and over. This rate sat between 66 percent and 67 percent from 1990 until 2008.

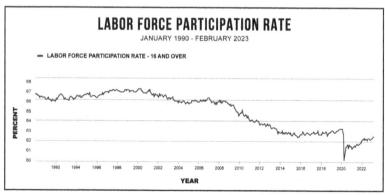

St. Louis Fed Economic Data, March 10, 2023

A few caveats are in order. Pre-1990 numbers are not used here for the simple reason that the 1950s and 1960s reflect a labor force with very few women in the workforce, and the 1970s and 1980s reflect the decades where that was dramatically changing (a significant diagonal line up to that 67 percent level). Our analysis begins at the point where there was a fairly consistent level of women in the workforce, so as to avoid comparisons between categorically different workforces. The 1950s and 1960s saw a roughly 60 percent labor participation rate, and the 1970s saw that jump to 64 percent. In the 1980s, it rose to the 67 percent rate at which it leveled off in 1990. This starting point reflects the normalized participation of women in the workforce.

Let's also address the impact of demography. The oft-discussed "baby boomer" demographic refers to those born post-World War II, between 1946 and 1964. In the first decade of this new century, baby boomers began turning fifty-five, and a "retirement boom" loomed as many in that demographic approached "retirement" age. (I will address some of my concerns with this assumption more in chapter 7.) We might be tempted to explain away a declining labor force demographically: because more babies were born from 1946 to 1964 than from 1965 to 1998, one could argue that there are more adults ages fifty-eight and over now retiring than there are adults in the "prime working years" of their life (ages twenty-five to fifty-four).

I want to make three points about what I see as the disaster of the labor participation rate decline:

We have a crisis of a declining participation rate in workers of pre-prime working age (ages sixteen to twenty-four).

We have a crisis of declining workers of prime working age (ages twenty-five to fifty-four).

That we have more people over the age of fifty-five now than we once did does not address the problem of fewer people ages fifty-five and over in the workforce. In other words, saying, "We don't need to worry about older people leaving the workforce because those people are older," is not as good a rebuttal as people think it is.

Demographics can be and should be unpacked here, but my *principle*, indisputable point—that our labor participation rate has dropped significantly—is not explicable by demographics alone. When we look at the three different age groups defined above, all invite concern. Let's look at each of them in turn.

I will begin with the labor participation rate of the youngest demographic measured in the data, those ages sixteen to twenty-four. The 1990 68 percent labor participation rate in this age demographic has dropped to 55–56 percent. This decline began at the turn of the century and accelerated after the 2008 Global Financial Crisis (GFC). It has stayed relatively level since the crisis, rising modestly before leveling off for the decade before COVID, collapsing during the pandemic (for obvious reasons), and now recovering to pre-COVID levels. But what is not close to being reached, and shows no signs it ever will, is the pre-GFC level of labor participation in those ages sixteen to twenty-four.

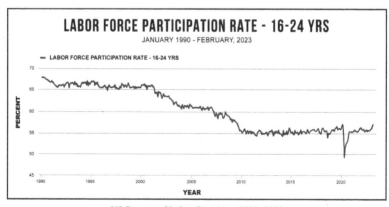

US Bureau of Labor Statistics, 1990–2023

The participation rate of prime-working-age people is a story all its own. Those who see those over fifty-five retiring as inconsequential and those under twenty-four waiting to start their careers as positive still may do a double take when they see the data for prime-working-age workers.

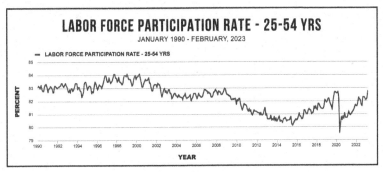

St. Louis Fed Economic Data, March 10, 2023

The data here is interesting, as we see a pre-GFC decline and a post-GFC collapse. Unlike in the chart for ages sixteen to twenty-four, we see a significant improvement for this latter demographic in the decade before COVID and have seen a stronger recovery post-COVID. That this participation rate is still down 1 percent from its level at the turn of the century means we remain down by 1.4 million workers in this core demographic.

The statistics for those over the age of fifty-five are intriguing, too. This participation force increased in the 1990s and 2000s because of the huge number of baby boomers entering the fifty-five-age range and still working. The absolute level in the rate remained low relative to other age ranges for the obvious reason that very few people over seventy still work, let alone those seventy-five, eighty, and eighty-five (even as life expectancy has increased throughout this time period). The rate stayed flat post-financial crisis, unlike the other two age groups we are analyzing, then collapsed during COVID and has not bounced back. The post-COVID data is most interesting to sociologists and economists for the fifty-five-plus demographic, for reasons we will highlight in a moment.

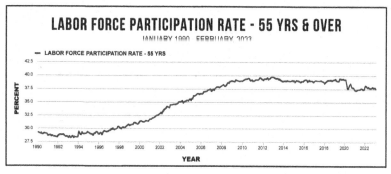

St. Louis Fed Economic Data, March 10, 2023

Across these age groups there is one problem that is easy to identify: *fewer people in the population are choosing to work, regardless of age and regardless of reason.*

While it's a single problem, the multi-variance here is import-ant—my concern for those not working at twenty-one is differ-ent than my concern for those not working at sixty-one. These distinctions and nuances will be important as we work through a cogent analysis of the data and how it speaks to the larger cultural epidemic.

Pre-Prime Working Age (Ages Sixteen to Twenty-Four)

First, let's examine trends in people ages sixteen to twenty-four. These ages count in the denominator of the participation rate ("working-age population"), and even though this tells a differ-ent story than the other age groups, it's a crucially important one. The decline in the labor participation rate of this younger demographic rate is exhibit A against the assertion that our total labor force decline can be explained away by baby boomers retiring.

In certain situations, it can be a good thing for high school students who do not need a job to focus on their studies and sports. Also, it is sometimes beneficial (or at least less problematic) for college students not to take a job and instead prioritize academics. But, more broadly, let's consider whether we view a substantially declining role in the labor force (having a job, or even wanting one) to be a good thing in each of the following populations:

High school students looking for part-time work for pocket money, but priced out by high minimum-wage jobs

High school students needing to save for post-high school life (college or otherwise), in addition to earning supplemental spending money

High school students looking for a way to learn basic job skills, including working for a boss and developing rapport with coworkers

College students seeking to avoid credit card debt as they work their way through college

College students seeking to minimize student loan debt

College students looking to earn pocket money and the ability to travel to see family over holidays

Young adults not in college seeking to pay living expenses or save for another objective (e.g., trade school or starting a business)

Young adults out of college or trade school who are ready to start adult life with a job

Those choosing to be supported by their parents (because they can) through their mid-twenties or later, rather than developing the independence and maturity that comes from financial self-sufficiency and earned success

Those delaying the procurement of an entry-level job or some form of early-stage career inception

Those at any circumstance, age, or educational attainment between the ages of sixteen and twenty-four who will enter the job market at twenty-five (or older) without ever having learned how to deal with a difficult boss; how to cooperate as part of a team; how to perform basic, remedial tasks; how to interact with customers; how to develop the discipline to show up on time; how to deal with the aggravation of being where you don't want to be; or how to achieve a goal or complete a project outside the classroom

In each of these scenarios, there are reasons not to celebrate the decline in "young adult" working. Of course, there are distinctions to be made, e.g., between age sixteen and age twenty-four; between those who need the money and those who do not; between those in college and those not in college. But on a macro level—without analyzing each individual situation and its particular circumstances—I view the scenarios bulleted above as ample illustration of why we should be alarmed by this massive decline of participation by those ages sixteen to twenty-four in the labor force, and should advocate for a robust increase in teen, college age, and young adult employment.

I view the last bullet as a matter of universal concern. Regardless of precise age, income, or circumstances, there is an undeniable benefit to working during those years. Life skills, experience, resilience, rejection, success, development of a mutual cooperation instinct, the basic practice of showing up, having responsibilities and expectations—all of these things form a certain *professional grammar* that will be deeply valuable throughout one's adult life, regardless of career.

Why have these participation rate numbers collapsed as they have? As the chart demonstrates, these levels didn't just drop during the financial crisis. The rate had been decreasing steadily in the decade preceding the GFC.

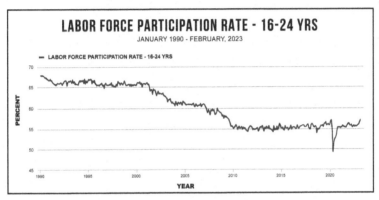

US Bureau of Labor Statistics, 1990–2023

The first economic shift driving the downward trend in young adult employment was the vast increase in those using student loans for non-tuition expenses. The view that student loans could be a source of spending money and bill support was held by roughly 20 percent of borrowers in the late 1990s/early 2000s, compared to over 30 percent by 2011.[18]

Additionally, minimum wage barriers exploded over this time period. The $4.25 per hour federal minimum wage I made in the early 1990s at Edwards Movie Theater was $7.25 by 2009 (a 71 percent increase). Practically speaking, with thirty states

---

18 New America Education Policy, Kim Dancy and Ben Barrett, *Living on Credit?*, August 2018, p. 15

now having a higher minimum wage than the federal minimum, including several above $15 per hour and over half over $10 per hour,[19] there is simply a higher barrier to entry for teens seeking employment. Though I certainly have opinions about the efficacy and propriety of minimum wage legislation, especially at the federal level, my point here is unrelated to the wisdom of the policy. It is an objective reality that rising minimum wages have depressed hiring of teens and across the entire lower-skilled segment of the labor force.

The arguments for higher labor participation in younger adults are numerous and persuasive. It would reduce student debt balances upon college graduation. It would reduce the burden of credit card debt so common for people in this age group. It would provide the qualitative benefits outlined above, in terms of both personal discipline and professional experience.

And finally, *it would lead to higher employment in the prime-working-age demographic.* Those who work for a meaningful portion of those eight years are more likely to work after age twenty-five, keep a job, and secure a new job should they lose one. Resilience and personal responsibility carry over to new spheres of professional industry. I do not use the techniques I honed tearing movie theater tickets in my career as a portfolio manager, but I have never forgotten what I learned while cleaning up dirty movie theater floors between shows: sometimes work means doing what you have to do, not what you want.

The infantilization of so many young men is linked to these labor statistics. The result is all around us: grown men who live as if they were children, addicted to video games and other vices, completely dependent on parental support economically and emotionally, devoid of real connection or responsibility. This

---

19   Economic Policy Institute, Minimum Wage Tracker, March 26, 2023.

result points to the cause: an abandonment of work and the cessation of a cultural condition that stigmatizes such abandonment.

We should find the decrease in labor participation amongst young adults unacceptable, and, by extension, the cultural and policy conditions that exacerbate it. It is a national tragedy that impacts not only our economic productivity (more on that shortly) but our collective and individual psychological and spiritual condition as well.

Post-Prime Working Age (Ages Fifty-Five Plus)

I will skip ahead to cover the fifty-five-plus demographic before coming back to the prime-working-age demographic. This has more to do with the effect a declining participation rate in this age group has on society than it does on the "decliners" themselves.

I take as a given that (most of the time) someone deciding to exit the workforce at age sixty-one has the financial means to do so. The costs when departures in this age bracket rise above what I call "organic" or "healthy" levels include lost mentorship, experience, and maturity. If one who has a potential three good years left leaves the workforce at sixty-two rather than sixty-five, what is the cost of those three lost years (net of the value received from the person replacing them)? This can't be assessed quantitatively, but we can assume there is a very real cost when the most experienced and most mature are no longer at their station.

I am sympathetic to the argument that sometimes an older person may be replaced by someone with higher physical and mental capacity. Plenty of pro sports teams have regretted seeing their salary cap eaten up by the bloated contracts of players past their prime. But assessment in the marketplace is far trickier than it is on the playing field. The physical requirements of most (not all) jobs are categorically different, and mental capability is often a positive for a sixty-year-old versus a thirty-year-old. This is not an issue of IQ but of experience, wisdom, and maturity. There are, for many vocational positions, benefits that come with age—with having experienced a variety of conditions and situations and being able to bring that perspective to new situations as they arise. There is no universal conclusion to come to here, other than that when those in the fifty-five-plus segment of the workforce depart, they take value with them.

Prime Working Age (Ages Twenty-Five to Fifty-Four)

Now, let's turn our attention to the prime-working-age demographic. First, let's revisit the labor force participation chart of this demographic:

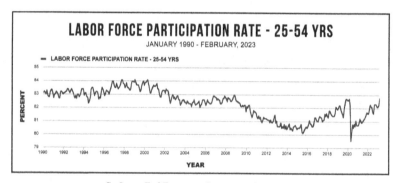

St. Louis Fed Economic Data, March 10, 2023

Some would argue that a 1–1.5 percent decline is not particularly significant. I would respond that we are talking about nearly 1.5 million people. And a deeper look reveals a worse problem than the surface-level data initially indicates.

Ninety-four percent of prime-aged men worked during the first twenty years after World War II. The number of men without work is now roughly 16 percent—one in six prime-aged men are without employment or wages.[20] We know more women have jobs now, but that is already covered in the total workforce and the working population figures.

The question is not just "Who has jobs?"—it is also, "What are people without jobs doing?" Sixteen percent of prime-working-age men are not in the workforce, and understanding what they are doing should be far more of a priority.

How concerning is that number? We did not collect employment data before World War II, but we do have the 1940 census to guide us. That census data shows nearly 14 percent of prime-aged men out of the workforce and an unemployment rate at 15 percent during the Great Depression. This means that *the work rate for prime-aged men this last decade is lower than it was in the Great Depression!* Does that not chill you to the bone?

The difference between now and the Great Depression is that we are not talking about joblessness—unemployment because there are no jobs—but rather a voluntary exit from the labor force. Voluntary worklessness provokes no outrage or policy interventions, but are the societal consequences any less concerning? This is the reason I am focused on the labor participation rate more than the unemployment rate. The latter does not capture the metric that I believe matters most—*the number of those not working.*

---

20   Dr. Nicholas Eberstadt, *Men Without Work*, Templeton Press, 2022, p. 7.

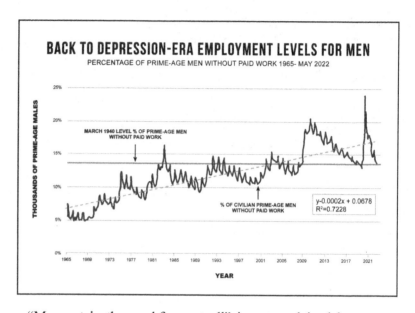

BACK TO DEPRESSION-ERA EMPLOYMENT LEVELS FOR MEN
PERCENTAGE OF PRIME-AGE MEN WITHOUT PAID WORK 1965- MAY 2022

"Men not in the workforce at all" is not explained by more women in the workforce, and it is not explained by a high unemployment rate (which we don't have). What we have is an exploding rate of men "not in the labor force"—a statistic that has been consistently rising over the last generation, unlike the statistic of "unemployed" men, which generally varies with economic conditions. Again, the difference is that to count as "unemployed" you have to be in the labor force, meaning employed "or desiring to be employed." The dumbfounding metric that warrants our analysis is primarily those prime-working-age men who have left the workforce all together.

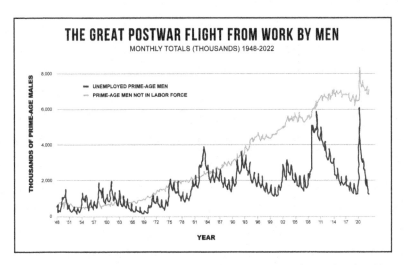

The growth in this metric is one of the rare consistencies in all labor economics. During recent economic recoveries, expansions, flatlinings, slowdowns, and contractions, the one commonality is an increase in men leaving the workforce.

These numbers include plenty of innocuous workforce departures, no doubt. There are plenty of legitimate, and even positive, reasons one may leave the workforce, but none of those are likely to be systemic, monolithic, and broad.

A mismatch of needed skills and available job positions is a haunting reality in labor markets, but not one that lacks a resolution. A lot of low-skill work has been outsourced, whether technologically or geographically, resulting in an unmet need of greater labor dynamism. Technological disruptions are not new, but a strong opposition to meeting the disruptions with new training and preparation is. We simply have not risen to meet this crisis, and instead are relying on state solutions that arguably exacerbate the problem.

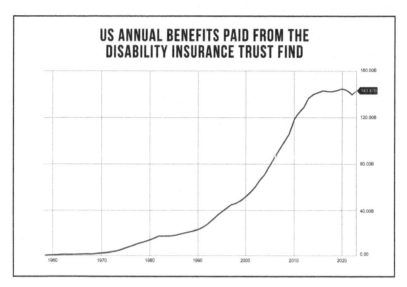

US ANNUAL BENEFITS PAID FROM THE DISABILITY INSURANCE TRUST FIND

The explosion of payouts in federal disability claims through the Social Security system does not mirror an explosion in private disability claims, and we have no centralized network offering data on the "true prevalence of disability recipience."[21] What we can say with certainty is that private disability costs and premiums have skyrocketed, and that carriers have no qualms about telling policyholders and new policy applicants that the reason is the increase in disability policy claims.

I do believe there is a mismatch of skills and available work in many cases, but I do not believe there is a mismatch of skill potential and available work. Many job openings require no college degree and, in fact, nearly 40 percent of non-working, prime-age men have a college degree.[22] Millions of jobs can be

---

21 Dr. Nicholas Eberstadt, *Men Without Work*, Templeton Press, 2022, p. 14. This is as good a spot as any to offer my gratitude for the extraordinary work of Dr. Nicholas Eberstadt, whose *Men Without Work* is a peerless encyclopedia of data and support establishing the crisis we have in voluntary worklessness.

22 Ibid, p. 18.

filled by any able-bodied person who wants a job, will show up on time, and can pass a drug test. That is a low bar for a society desperately in need of more workers.

If our work rate were the same today as it was in 2000, an additional ten million Americans would be working.[23] Imagine the increase in production of goods and services that ten million more workers would spur. Imagine the downward pressure on inflation such an increase in supply would create. The decline in the rate of GDP growth since these labor statistics changed is striking. We are $6 trillion below the trend line level of post-war economic growth since the year 2000 (an aggregate diminishment of 25 percent of GDP below what it would be over the last twenty-three years if the growth rate of the prior fifty years had been maintained).[24]

Would this extra $48,000 per household be useful in current economic times?[25] How have income inequality and wealth inequality been exacerbated by this declining labor participation? How does millions of people not working impact total contributions to Social Security and Medicare, the two largest unfunded liabilities in American history?

What has the impact on our productivity been? Labor productivity grew 2.2 percent on average for the seventy years after World War II. It has not been even close to that rate in well over a decade! We have better technology, better artificial intelligence, and better access to capital than ever before, yet productivity is falling. Declining workforce output and participation are taking a toll on economic opportunity.

---

23   Ibid, p. 6.
24   Ibid, p. 6.
25   Calculated as $6 trillion dividend by the 124 million households of the 2021 Census Bureau.

The purpose of this book is much more than begging those not working to reconsider their decisions. I want to argue for a particular attitude towards work and an understanding of calling and ambition that hopefully speaks to many people with jobs, just as I hope it will resonate with people without jobs. But if there were any doubt that our overall attitude towards work needs reform, the case is fortified by the economic and cultural reality I have described in this chapter.

Please do not misunderstand what I am saying here. There are certainly people who "leave the workforce" for legitimate reasons. The dynamic nature of the American economy allows for many different situations and types of activity. But the trends, absolute numbers, and changes in ratios over time are too compelling to ignore an obvious message: *We have an epidemic of worklessness, primarily in men, with different negative consequences depending on which demographic group we are talking about.*

Whether we are referring to young adults, the over-fifty-five group, or those in their prime-working-age period of life, the data is troubling. It speaks to a broad cultural reality that is eroding economic growth, suffocating productivity, and cutting people off from their God-created purpose.

That God-created purpose is the subject of our next chapter.

CREATED FOR WHAT?

WHAT GENESIS REALLY SAYS ABOUT WORK

MOVIE THEATER USHER

The Church's approach to an intelligent carpenter is usually confined to exhorting him not to be drunk and disorderly in his leisure hours, and to come to church on Sundays. What the Church should be telling him is this: that the very first demand that his religion makes upon him is that he should make good tables.

—Dorothy Sayers

The arguments that work is a needed antidote to the loneliness and despair of our day (covered in chapter 1) and that a decrease in labor participation is damaging economic productivity (chapter 2) are inadequate without the argument I make in this chapter. If I have gotten the theology and teleology wrong, pragmatic and practical considerations pack much less of a punch. Indeed, many things with therapeutic benefits might not be healthy, constructive, or commanded. My arguments in the preceding chapters must be tethered to creational truth, which is our objective in this chapter.

To get right to the point, I believe it is abundantly clear from the plain teaching of Scripture that God created mankind *for the purpose of work*. We must not be content with a theological framework that merely allows for work, encourages a certain kind of work, or offers broadly positive sentiments about work. Rather, we must recognize that from the very creation of mankind, God intended us to be workers, producers, and agents of growth and dominion. He connected our identity to our work. He established our telos—our purpose—as cultivators of creation. He called for a flourishing garden—a productive and beautiful place where our work does important things. God did all this.

We fail to appreciate this Genesis account of work at our own peril.

In the Beginning

Let us start where I often recommend Christians start in understanding the Bible: Genesis 1. Those who know Christian theology know that Genesis 1 comprises the first passages of the Bible, the very account of God creating man. Notably, it takes place before the fall, that moment of "original sin" that forever changed history and created our desperate need for redemption. Our views of work, our interpretation of work, our understanding of meaning and how it applies to all fields of work—all take place in the context of this fallen (sinful) world. We will have much to say about the post-fall reality of work and its effect on human destiny and purpose.

But before we can look at the ramifications of sin for work it behooves us to understand the pre-fall truth about work. What can we learn from Genesis 1 that we can carry into our modern understanding of our own purpose and calling? What aspects of the creational truths of Genesis 1 are relevant to the subject at hand?

Very Good

I have often commented on the profundity of a certain adjective that exists in the creation account. After twenty-five straight verses describing the five days of creation, with the product of each day described as "good," we arrive at the sixth day of the creation account (verse 26). He explains His intentions for what He created in verses 26–30, the verses we will unpack next. But then the chapter ends with verse 31 and the inclusion of a powerful adjective that was noticeably absent in each of the preceding verses. What God created on day six was not described merely as *good*—that was the adjective used to describe things like land, water, and vegetation; stars, the sun, and the moon; and birds, fish, and animals. Rather, what God created on day six was *very good*. And what was it that warranted this modifier not applied to the wonders of the oceans and the skies?

Mankind. God made mankind, and mankind alone, as *very* good. What was the reason for this elevated status? What characteristics does mankind possess that account for man and woman being described by the Creator as *very good*?

I will argue that this elevated status is directly linked to the human capacity for productive, creative, and innovative work. And I will make this argument exegetically, letting the Bible speak for itself.

Creation Mandate

I previously stated that verses 1–25 of Genesis 1 describe the first five days of creation, building up to the grand finale. Verses 26–28 describe the creation of mankind, and the final verse of the chapter (31) gives us the "very good" description. Let's take a closer look at the verses that provide the foundational theology for mankind's purpose:

> Then God said, "Let us make mankind **in our image, in our likeness,** *so that* **they may rule over the fish in the sea and the birds in the sky, over the livestock and all the wild animals, and over all the creatures that move along the ground."**

> So God created mankind **in his own image, in the image of God** he created them; male and female he created them.

> **God blessed them** and said to them, "**Be fruitful and increase in number; fill the earth and subdue it. Rule over** the fish in the sea and the birds in the sky and over **every living creature** that moves on the ground." (NIV)

The emphases added above are mine, highlighting the points most relevant to our study. It is stated no fewer than four times in just two verses that mankind was made in the image and likeness of God. God made us with dignity, and that dignity is delineated in the context of mankind as steward, cultivator, and ruler. He gave a rather sweeping objective in describing *their very purpose in having been created*—to be fruitful, grow, increase, fill, subdue. What these verses lay out can be described theologically as an "economic growth" mandate.

From Sand to the iPhone

It is in Genesis 2 that we get more "play-by-play" of the sixth day of creation. The picture is painted of a garden God created (v. 8) between rivers He also created (v. 10), with vivid descriptions of the beauty, potential, and needs of the garden (vv. 9, 11, 12). In verse 15, once again:

The Lord God took the man and put him in the Garden of Eden **to work it and take care of it.** (NIV)

Mankind's ability to act as an image-bearer of God is directly tied to the mandate God gives: *that they work to cultivate the potential of creation.* God's created world was intentionally created unfinished, and mankind (made in the image and likeness of God) was entrusted with transforming that potential into the actual. The verb that best captures actualizing the potential of creation is, well, *work.*

The Human Things

We are provided a clear picture of humans working to care for and steward this creation, and in so doing to fill the earth. This population mandate is entirely economic—God made us with certain needs and wants, and tasked us with ruling over this process of increase and extraction. If we are to understand the depth of this created reality, it behooves us to understand the nature of the human person.

God made the world with *design*, and it reflects His creative talent as the *designer*. He made us in His image, planting a desire in mankind (the created) to become a cocreator (as an image-bearer of God). In making us the sole object of creation capable of seeing and creating beauty, He manifested this image-bearing reality of mankind-as-designer. Of course, we cannot create ex nihilo, as God alone can (that is, "out of nothing"). But, our creative nature can honor the beautiful in creation and allows us to create from the raw materials of the earth. Music, sculpture, painting, architecture, and all great forms of art represent humans as designers, working with the canvas of creation provided to us by God.

We are more than just artists and designers. We are human beings created with reason and rationality. We respond to incentives, possess a strong sense of self-preservation, and have a high capacity for understanding. Our awareness transcends mere stimuli and signals and encompasses a capacity for truly conceptual thought. We can see more than what our basic sensory functions perceive. In this sense, we are *thinkers* and capable of great *strategy*. Our intellect aligns with the transcendent. This flows from entirely unique human characteristics given to us by our Creator.

We have a capacity for self-reflection, for interiority. We are conscious beings with thoughts, emotions, and imaginations. We experience joy and disappointment, glory and failure, fear and love. For this reason, a human must never be described only in his or her capacity for working, *or* as just a sort of subconscious being. We were created with both material and spiritual dimensions, *all before sin entered the world*. And this dual reality of human materiality and spirituality was described as *very good*.

Ancient Heresy

The fatal error of Gnosticism is to view the immaterial as morally and transcendently superior to the physical. The theology of the Bible does not present this false binary! Interiority is a key aspect of humanity, and each man and woman has a soul that will never die—and so, an eternal destiny. But we also have a physical body and exist in a material universe. We were placed at creation in a garden—a place of scarcity and vulnerability, yes, but also beauty, potential, and the need for stewardship.

It is a Gnostic heresy to view the creation account as God making the human person only for spiritual fulfillment and heavenly companionship. Those immaterial realities reflect a fundamental part of the human person, but not the entirety. In the materiality of humanity lies a capacity for work, for productive labor, for stewardship, for innovation, for creative design, and, yes, for growth. Over time, we began to speak of this process as "wealth"—that is, the goods and services that enhance our quality of life and serve the needs of humanity.

Basic Vocabulary

What else is wealth? Is it the accumulation of shiny gold coins that sit in a drawer, devoid of any substantive value to one's standard of living? Is it paper money entered in some type of bank record, or cash under a mattress? Or, rather, is it the goods and services that we may acquire through a medium of exchange known as money?

No rational person would describe a person living in abject poverty and distress as "wealthy" just because they had a unit of account somewhere tallied on a ledger or stored in their shoebox. These units of account represent wealth only to the extent that they can be exchanged for goods and services—the goods and services that we refer to as wealth creation.

Wealthy societies have abundant goods and services that enable a higher standard of living. They acquire those goods and services (and have acquired them over millennia) *by work*. That is what work is: the production of goods and services that meet the needs of humanity. Wealthy societies build, grow, develop, cultivate, and steward. Poor societies do not. This was true at the Garden of Eden and is still true today. There is one verb that drives wealth—*work*, the verb of economics.

Man for Work and Work for Man

The theological construct is that work is the purpose of the human person, ordained as such by God, and that the objects of these endeavors are other people who benefit from them. Service is a necessary component of work. This reality speaks to another key component of humankind—that we are created in a familial, social, and communal context. We flourish in relationship with other people. Our existence is not merely for the good of society—our dignity is bestowed upon as individuals made in the image of God—and yet we are called to community. There is profound meaning in this as it pertains to the creation mandate of work.

The ontological reality of human dignity and human destiny is that each of our lives both has meaning individually and brings meaning to the lives of those around us. People are not objects for our use, but rather subjects in the story of life. Pope John Paul II elucidated this in his masterful *Laborem Exercens* when he said that work is a transitive activity, i.e., it begins with a human subject (us) and is then directed toward an external object (others).[26] We honor this God-created reality in our work—we as workers are the subject and the rest of mankind is the object. In this subjective dimension we find the source of dignity in our work. The value of work rests in the fact that the worker is a human being created by God in His image with dignity and value.[27]

In a holistic and creational understanding of work, we see at once the *individual* and *relational* dynamic of the human person on display. God made us with an innate purpose to work (individual meaning), and this brings with it an inherent social value

---

26   Pope John Paul II, *Laborem Exercens*, September 14, 1981.

27   Ibid.

(our work serves the needs of others). This not only serves as a building block for a moral and efficient market economy, but it reflects a created reality of the human person.

Production, Not Acquisition

The ugly irony of the contemporary debate over the significance of work is that it is the pro-growth, pro-work, pro-productivity camp that is called "materialistic," when this worldview actually stems from a view of human nature that is anything but. In the worldview I am presenting, the inherent dignity of man stems from his status as an image-bearer of God who now is on earth to "cocreate" with Him (that is, to extract potential from the creation that God alone made ex nihilo). That dignity is unrelated to an accumulation of possessions or status. Furthermore, if work ceases to serve others, there is no demand for it. We cannot earn our daily bread without delivering value. There is a material provision to the worker and to those who benefit from their work, yes, but that is by no means the full extent of the value. This vision for work "corresponds to man's dignity...expresses this dignity, and increases it."[28] From the created order, we see that work was designed not only to meet the material needs of mankind but to provide fulfillment in our humanity.

Putting the Curse into Context

We examined Genesis 1 and 2 because they cover the creation account, and the purpose of this chapter is to evaluate what God created us for from the outset. The notion of human beings as possessing elevated dignity, sharing the image and fullness of the triune God, being individual and social, having a unique capacity for creativity, innovation, and productivity, and now

---

28   Ibid.

charged with cultivating, stewarding, inhabiting, and growing, is all established from the creation of the world, and yet before the fall of man (sin entering the world), which is chronicled in Genesis 3. Some have dared to suggest that at the point of the fall the story changed—that work became a curse, not a blessing. The text itself and the theology behind this warrant a closer look.

After the original sin occurred (Adam and Eve eating from the tree of the knowledge of good and evil), God confronted His creation in the garden. After the normal blame-casting and fin-ger-pointing that has accompanied sin ever since, Adam and Eve were left guilty and ashamed, and God doled out the curses that would plague them and their offspring going forward:

> To the woman he said,
>
> "I will make your pains in childbearing very severe; with painful labor you will give birth to children. Your desire will be for your husband, and he will rule over you."
>
> To Adam he said, "Because you listened to your wife and ate fruit from the tree about which I commanded you, 'You must not eat from it,'
>
> "Cursed is the ground because of you; through painful toil you will eat food from it all the days of your life. It will produce thorns and thistles for you, and you will eat the plants of the field. By the sweat of your brow you will eat your food until you return to the ground, since from it you were taken; for dust you are and to dust you will return." (NIV)

The first point that must be made about verses 17–19 is that if they do, indeed, mean that all work is now a curse in a sinful world, verse 16 implies that children and husbands are a curse, too. Do we believe that the pain of childbirth (and complexities of the pregnancy process implied in this passage) speak to the curse being children themselves? Scripture itself refutes this concept explicitly over and over again:

"Children are a gift from the Lord, a reward from Him."
—Psalm 127:3 (NLT)

"Children's children are a crown to the aged."
—Proverbs 17:6 (NIV)

"Before I formed you in the womb I knew you, before you were born I set you apart. —Jeremiah 1:5 (NIV)

"Discipline your children, and they will give you peace and make your heart glad." —Proverbs 29:17 (NLT)

Interestingly, the very point I am making (that the curse refers to the pain of childbirth, but the actual child is a pure blessing) is explicitly anticipated and stated in John 16:21 (NIV):

A woman giving birth to a child has pain because her time has come; but when her baby is born she forgets the anguish because of her joy that a child is born into the world.

Throughout history, no one has interpreted the curse of the garden to mean that babies are a curse or that children produce misery. And yet that is often what people interpret verses 17–19 to say about work. In Genesis 1 and 2, God made work fundamental to the purpose and nature of man, yet we are to believe that in Genesis 3 the very idea of work becomes a curse? It is a logically and theologically incoherent idea. Just as the preceding verse added the pain of childbirth to the process of a child being born, work is now accompanied by toil, struggle, and sweat. The framework for reconciling this tension is provided in the curse given to Eve—as childbirth comes with great pain and yet children are a blessing, so is work a great blessing, even when accompanied (because of the curse of sin) by stress, anxiety, and physical pain.

But the next step of our task hermeneutically is not just to see the parallels between these two curses, but to understand the very essence of Christian theology itself. God's intent for His world was severely impacted by sin, but it did not end there. The fundamental message of the Christian religion is that God redeems His people to Himself. We know the gospel message is that He did this through the work of His Son on the cross, where He paid the penalty for us all and conquered sin and death through the glory of the resurrection. We live now through this redemptive process, whereby God restores that which sin has torn down. He makes beauty from ashes, and what was old becomes new again.

Sin caused Adam and Eve to abuse their stewardship of God's creation, but Christ's redemptive work now calls us to a restored notion of stewardship—the notion announced in the Garden at the very creation of the world. On this side of glory, it is tainted by sin and subject to the curse (pain, toil, distress). All the while, it is being made new and perfect again through the process of redemption that we call "history."

This is what we are living through—a period of redemption and restoration that is the covenantal promise of God. Through this period of redemption, we work. We work because we were created to do so, and because in our work we reflect the image of God, who transforms the ugly into the beautiful. Our work becomes a venue of this redemption, as is His entire Kingdom. We find a glimmer of the new life, the garden, and the promise of a celestial city in our work.

The Seventh Day

I would fail miserably to faithfully exegete the creation account if I only remembered the six days wherein God worked, created, and produced. Our society's obsession with vacation, rest, and "self-care" is directly correlated to a lost understanding of real Sabbath rest. This unbalanced view is inevitable when we lose sight of the creation model for work and rest—that is, six days of work and one day of rest.

If I wrote a book calling us to imitate God in work but not in rest, I would be failing to tell the whole Genesis story. God has called us to be image-bearers of Him in both work *and rest*. His version of rest does not call for extended naps, yoga sessions, or hour-long coffee breaks throughout the workday, though. The modern obsession with infantilizing adult workers is the result of forfeited Sabbath theology. We work for six days and rest for one, as God did. The only two theological points of interest here are that:

1. God rested and so must we.
2. His proportionality was six to one.

I have little interest in unpacking much beyond that. Those two components are a solid starting place for developing limits on our society's boundless desire for relaxation. In point number one, I offer up a Biblical command, not an option. In point number two, I seek to provide a mathematical construct. Beyond those two points, I will refrain from specific application. The principles ought to be enough: God rested, and He did so one day out of seven.

Conclusion

Being an image-bearer of God is to carry the attributes of God that He chose to share with us, key among them creativity and productivity. It is not merely a blessing but a duty. We work because God worked, and in working we find purpose and calling. We work in recognition of the fact that God has equipped us to do great things, by extracting potential from the created (material) world and combining that physical dimension with our ideas, imagination, and innovations, resulting in growth, cultivation, and stewardship.

Dominion over creation is a duty to care—a responsibility to preserve and grow. This has always required a social context, and in the modern world, it involves work for and service to a variety of economic actors, including employers, employees, investors, vendors, customers, suppliers, and more. The division of labor whereby we bring our unique and specialized gifts to various projects has enabled incredible human flourishing. The modern miracle of specialization and division of labor is a byproduct of creation—of God making us unique, special, and individually distinct, with each carrying his or her own passions and talents. All of this is brought to what we call "work," and all of it began at creation.

I leave you with the opening words of the *Laborem Exercens* encyclical from Pope John Paul II, written a generation ago. Few documents have better captured how the essence of creation theology applies to work. Our understanding of work must reconnect to creation theology and realign with a Biblical understanding of us as created *imago dei*. That understanding feeds a true appreciation for work as inherent to the purpose and meaning of mankind.

> *Through work man must earn his daily bread and contribute to the continual advance of science and technology and, above all, to elevating unceasingly the cultural and moral level of the society within which he lives in community with those who belong to the same family. And work means any activity by man, whether manual or intellectual, whatever its nature or circumstances; it means any human activity that can and must be recognized as work, in the midst of all the many activities of which man is capable and to which he is predisposed by his very nature, by virtue of humanity itself. Man is made to be in the visible universe an image and likeness of God himself, and he is placed in it in order to subdue the earth. From the beginning therefore he is called to work. Work is one of the characteristics that distinguish man from the rest of creatures, whose activity for sustaining their lives cannot be called work. Only man is capable of work, and only man works, at the same time by work occupying his existence on earth. Thus work bears a particular mark of man and of humanity, the mark of a person operating within a community of persons. And this mark decides its interior characteristics; in a sense it constitutes its very nature.*[29]

---

29   Ibid.

THE SERMON YOU'LL NEVER HEAR

THE WHOLE BIBLE'S MESSAGE ON WORK

SIZZLER SERVER

If you want to produce Christian work, be a Christian,
and try to make a work of beauty into which you have
put your heart; do not adopt a Christian pose.

—*Jacques Maritain*

Mankind's basic purpose is found in the book of Genesis. Chapter 3 of this book used creational theology from the beginning of Scripture to set the stage for the Bible's teachings on the subject of work. Genesis is the "beginning" (by definition) but by no means the end, and there is much more to say about our theological understanding of work.

I will use chapter 9 to evaluate pastors and their approach to their own work, which surely colors their teachings on the subject (more often for bad than for good, I'll argue). My aim in this chapter is to assess what is being missed in contemporary church teaching about work. The creational realities of the prior chapter are at the top of that list. Do I believe modern pastors are unaware of the basic Christian anthropology laid out in chapter 3? Of course not. The main thrust of these creational truths is known but ignored, available but dismissed, powerful but threatening.

In this chapter, I will expand upon the Bible's teachings about work beyond the lessons of Genesis 1. I want to examine why foundational understandings (creational theology) and additive exposition and application are rarely the subject of Sunday-morning sermons. I am going to suggest that there may be a theological deficiency at play, a closet pact with an ancient heresy, and an underlying conflict of interests. Whether today's ecclesial messages on work are driven by one of these three or a combination thereof, my aim in this chapter is to point us to a better place, convicted by shortcomings up until now, and filled with ambitions for a more faithful presentation of this monumentally important topic.

(Dis)Comfort Level

How many pastors today would feel comfortable saying that our meaning in life comes from work? How many *should* feel comfortable saying that? Isn't it easier to say that our meaning comes from God, and that our obedience and service to God is the meaning of life? The Biblical message that God loves us and saved us by grace is true and clean, and it avoids the messiness of where I want to take this subject of meaning.

I believe we need to become comfortable with saying that our meaning comes from God (most pastors are on board here), *and* that our meaning comes from the work that we do—precisely because that is what God desires. For a pastor to say the latter with conviction, they need first to understand the harmony between the two.

Discomfort comes from the belief that these two beliefs are at odds with each other. If deriving meaning from work eliminated the meaning, dignity, and purpose we have as created by God, I, too, would be uncomfortable with such language. However, we do not face such a dilemma of "work versus God." Rather, we find our meaning in God, a worker, who made us in His image to worship Him. When we finally understand what this means, informed by the testimony of Scripture, we can conclude that our meaning is wrapped in God, which is to say, it is wrapped in work.

Work or Worship or Both?

The Hebrew word *avodah* (הָדוֹבֲע) is found in the Scriptures over four hundred times (either in the verb form, *avad*, or the noun form, *avodah*). The word is variously translated as "work," "worship," or "service" in English translations of the Bible, with translators doubtless led by context. When one word is translated as both "work" and "worship," we may be on to more of a harmony than we had previously thought. Can there be more harmony than two ideas sharing the same translated word? As we shall see, we are not dealing only with a fascinating translational reinforcement of this message, but also in the context itself, a powerful Biblical message.

We were first exposed to this word in Genesis 2:15 when we saw that mankind was made to work and take care of the Garden. The fourth commandment (Exodus 34:21 ESV) is unambiguous when it says:

> Six days you shall work, but on the seventh day you shall rest

This word undoubtedly refers to "work" (labor, vocation, etc.) because it is held in specific contrast to "rest," which is sort of the whole point of the commandment! The same can be said for Psalm 104:23 (NIV):

Then people go out to their work, to their labor
until evening

We gloss over the intricacies of the word if we think of "work" as
only referring to "nice Christian-ministry work." In Exodus 5:18,
we see it used in the context of Pharaoh asking the Israelites to
do manual labor in the fields. In Ezekiel 29:18, we see it applied
to the work of King Nebuchadnezzar's army. In Genesis 29:27,
it refers to work done for money. In Jeremiah 22:13, it refers to
work done apart from compensation. It also applies to work done
in a church context (Joshua 22:27, Numbers 3:8).[30] Every type
of work is covered—and the work is real-life work. It is *avodah*.

But: the exact same word is translated as "worship" in countless contexts, and "serve" in many others. Until I was doing the
research for this chapter, I didn't know that one of my favorite
verses in the Bible (Joshua 24:15 NIV) uses this word:

But if **serving the** Lord seems undesirable to you, then
choose for yourselves this day whom you will **serve**...
But as for me and my household, we will **serve** the Lord.

The same word is used to describe the explicit worship and
praise of God as is used to describe the basic function of work.
It is the Gnostic heresy that has separated the spiritual (worship)
from the material (work). *Avodah* does no such thing. Dualism
may be rampant in the pulpits, where the "sacred" (church) is
separated from the "secular" (work). *Avodah* unifies the sacred
and the secular. Our work is quite literally worship—actual
service—to God. Grammatically and theologically, ecclesial
attempts to separate our lives into the compartments of "work"
and "ministry"—the vocational versus the avocational—are

---

30   Dave Huber, "Avodah Word Study," Evangelical Free Church of America, ,
      Summer 2012.

flawed. When it comes to work and worship, only a message of integration passes the Biblical smell test.[31]

Two Verbs for the Price of One

Let's revisit Genesis 2:15 (NIV) once more.

> The Lord God took the man and put him in the Garden of Eden **to work it and take care of it.**

Avodah covers the English "to work it," but what about the second part, "take care of it" (other translations say to "keep" it)? The Hebrew word here is *shamar* (רָמַשׁ), which means "to exercise great care." It involves protection, watching over, preservation, and diligent guidance. The root word is used in hundreds of different contexts in the Bible, and furthers our understanding of work in the garden and in modern life. Far from "clocking in and clocking out," Adam and Eve were given work that required diligent care and oversight. The same passage is used throughout the Scripture to describe shepherds caring for their flock, guards protecting a city, and even God keeping us from danger. It is an all-encompassing root with a profound obligation for those receiving the command—our acts of work, stewardship, and cultivation—the ones we were created for.

The Consistent Theme of the Parables

Many pastors love unpacking the parables of Jesus, and for good reason. They're packed with both masterful messages of Biblical truth and powerful lessons in ethics and practical theology. They are relevant, timely, lasting, and reflect the pedagogical prowess of the greatest teacher the world has ever known.

---

31 Austin Burkhart, "Avodah: What It Means," Institute for Faith, Work, & Economics, March 31, 2015.

Father Robert Sirico of the Acton Institute recently pointed out that the parables contain timeless lessons in the broader subject of economics.[32] The wisdom one can find in these texts on matters as varied as family disputes, wealth distribution, and care for the poor is incomparable, all without imposing any views or expectations onto the text.

Yet in all of our appreciation of the parables, I encourage pastors and laymen alike to view them through the lens of vocation. Time and time again the Son-of-God-made-man uses vocation and work to illustrate profound spiritual truths. The foolish man who built his house on sand, the sower who scattered seeds across all types of ground, the seamstress sewing in different types of garments, the winemaker pouring into different wineskins, the farmer dealing with wheat and weeds, the bread-maker mixing flour into the bread, the merchant looking for pearls, the fisherman casting a net for fish in a lake, the shepherd searching for his missing sheep, the king settling accounts with his workers, the landowner hiring laborers for his vineyard, the rich man tearing down his barns to build for more grain— these are all stories of people with jobs and vocational significance (not always *prominence*, but always *significance*), where the spiritual lesson is inseparable from their work. These day-to-day affairs of economic activity (i.e., work) were the tools Jesus used in telling the great parables. Their status and context with various professions and responsibilities were not ignored or anecdotal but rather were the basis for lasting spiritual lessons.

His Workmanship

At first read, most people would not think Ephesians 2:10 (ESV) refers to work or vocation. After all, the focus is seemingly on

---

32   Father Robert Sirico, *The Economics of the Parables*, Regnery Gateway, 2022.

us being the created work of God, with a little additional language that seems to speak to our call to obedience:

> For we are His workmanship, created in Christ Jesus for good works, which God prepared beforehand that we should walk in them.

But wait, what were we created for? "Good works" surely means "those activities that are good," like helping our neighbor, being loving to our spouse, and assisting with a program to feed the homeless, right? We know that we are not saved *by* good works, but when we see Biblical language using those words, our minds presume something non-vocational.

It turns out that *ergois agathois* (ἔργοις ἀγαθοῖς) is an important choice of words in this Ephesians passage. The good work we are created to do, according to Paul, is indistinguishable from vocational work in translation. The words are literally what someone would say to describe high-quality work in their job. We were "created to do work that is good." This is not new information in the Pauline epistle; it was stated from the outset of creation in Genesis. I do not think the passage excludes non-vocational work, but interpreting it as excluding vocational work is terrible hermeneutics (and terrible Greek). Many other adjectives and nouns existed in Greek that specified broad acts of charitable service. The work we were created to do is described in the same grammar as economic and material labor. This "grammar" is needed in our pulpits.

Necessary but Not Sufficient

I commend any sermon focused on Christian obedience. Exhorting a congregation to "sin less" at work (or anywhere else) is noble and needed. But as Dorothy Sayers famously said, the carpenter needs to be told more at church than just not to be drunk or to come to church—he needs to be told to make good tables. It would take a whole other book to adequately address church teaching on sin and obedience, but for our purposes I contend that work itself has been considered spiritually insignificant, so churches have focused on the periphery. I believe we have this backwards.

Sermons should be given about ethical tensions at work. Christian piety and living matter. Obviously, our marriages, social interactions, and challenges in raising children deserve pulpit exhortation. That said, the spiritual significance of work and the attendant duties of the Christian in his or her occupation transcend the supplemental behaviors and relational realities we bring to work. There is also a Biblical command for competence and performance.

Sayers also said that "God is not served by technical incompetence; and incompetence and untruth always result when the secular vocation is treated as a thing alien to religion."[33] By my reading, the whole counsel of the Bible demands that ministers speak to the inherent meaning of our endeavors themselves.

Good Intentions

There is no doubt in my mind that many churches fail to fully capture the power of the Biblical message of work with good intentions, whether by basic theological ignorance or mere incompletion. They provide a message they know to be good ("church ministry work is valuable") and miss the part of the message that is of far more significance to their congregants ("your work is valuable; your work is part of God's Kingdom"). Too often, a closet dualism that separates the sacred and secular permeates the mentality of those behind the pulpits and, by

---

33   Dorothy Sayers, "Why Work?" *Letters to a Diminished Church*, 1942.

extension, those in the pews. Breaking out of this default position will not happen without intentional effort.

I do not want to give pastors a pass just because they have good intentions. Assuming that the predominant sin of the church is congregants working too hard defies common sense. Given any cultural awareness at all, pastors must be aware of the epidemic I described in chapters 1 and 2. The infantilization of young adult men, in particular, is so well-known that it has become the stuff of memes, skits, sitcoms, and movies. It is a theological choice by pastors to preach endlessly about the dangers of work, career, and professional ambitions when video game obsessions are a deeper cultural reality.[34]

My criticism is not that church messages on this issue start on the defensive—"You know, your jobs can be a good thing and they matter to God, but let's talk about how they aren't really your identity and you need to care about them a little less." My criticism is of the failure to recognize the reality that congregations almost certainly contain more people working too little than too much. And yet, the framing of the subject—the prima facie messaging—is to warn against that which is, at worst, a secondary matter, and very likely nonexistent altogether, while ignoring the systemic sins of sloth, nonproductivity, and irresponsibility.

Evangelical churches have seemingly grown incapable of leading with *praise* for hard work and *condemnation* of low productivity. If you ever heard this setup for a sermon, what would you expect the next point to be?

---

34 According to data analytics company Stream Hatchet, 1.6 billion hours of Fortnite were streamed last year from over eighty million registered users, 89.7 percent of which were men between the ages of eighteen and thirty-four.

Today I want to address those of you who are striving for the corner office, who worked late a couple of nights this week, who are receiving big bonuses and the praise of men, and yet are grinding, struggling, and fixating so much of the time on your jobs and careers.

Does anyone actually think if that were the setup that the next line would be something like this?

Well done! You are being faithful and obedient. I pray you are finding the joy in this worthy calling you are after, and I hope we can address in this sermon the Biblical commandments that we all behave that way, with ambition, diligence, excellence, and hustle!

Or do we all know that the next line would be something like this:

We must address the temptation to think that our work defines us and is the basis for our identity. We must check our motives and make sure that we are focused on generosity and giving, and not professional accolades and rewards.

That prioritization is what I am targeting in this chapter—the choice to pastorally prioritize something that is so uncommon over something so prevalent. If our churches better understood creational theology—the concept of *avodah* and the whole-Bible message about work, stewardship, and calling—would our first impulse be one of caution or one of celebration? Something has gone off the rails, and it is time we re-center the church's message on this topic to align with the impulse and priority of Scripture.

Generosity Properly Understood

It would be a grievous mistake to assume that I do not take generosity seriously. I not only believe it to be at the heart of the Christian life, but I have studied economics enough to know that those who work hard are often in a better position to be generous than those who do not (imagine that!). I certainly believe that the message of the widow who gave two mites (Luke 21:1-4) is incredibly important. Generosity is, above all else, a reflection of the heart. God loves a cheerful giver.

I celebrate a powerful message from our pulpits on the importance of generosity, as long as that message doesn't also devalue work and productivity. Different workers (stewards, cultivators, growers) will find themselves in different positions of financial capacity, and the Bible is clear about the corresponding quantitative requirements (tithes and offerings) and qualitative expectations (cheerful, sacrificial, heartfelt giving). We cannot advocate for a faithful sharing of the fruit from the tree without robust preaching in defense of the tree. Giving comes from first fruits, the fruits of our *labor*. To reduce work to the mere utilitarian benefit of generosity that may flow from work is to understand neither the purpose of work nor the definition of generosity.

One possible way to preach a more faithful message of generosity would be to focus on the anonymity—the lack of concern for credit and attention—that is supposed to be at the heart of Biblical giving. Self-aggrandizing public proclamations of personal generosity seem to be at the heart of evangelical messaging about giving these days. If you are a pastor tempted to have a big donor in your church come up to give a brief "testimonial" about how generous they chose to be, consider Matthew 6:1-6 and refrain.

But I digress. Generosity with one's time and financial resources is most certainly a wonderful and faithful thing, and it warrants exegesis from the pulpits. I would ask pastors who have somehow found every single message given on work and generosity: what do you *think* the implicit message has been? Likely, the whole point of the Luke 21 parable of the widow has been undermined. Churches are all too often implying, likely without intending to do so, that the burden of giving is the exclusive duty of the rich, when the Bible could not be clearer that this is not true. But beyond that, millions of churchgoing people have internalized that the purpose of their work is to have money from which they can give to ministry. This is not an accurate message about work or generosity, and it undermines a Biblical understanding of both.

A Conflict by Any Other Name

Dorothy Sayers hated dualism, and knew that the church faced a conflict that had to be overcome if we were to faithfully teach the Biblical message on work:

> It is the business of the Church to recognize that the secular vocation, as such, is sacred. Christian people, and particularly perhaps the Christian clergy, must get it firmly into their heads that when a man or woman is called to a particular job of secular work, that is as true a vocation as though he or she were called to specifically religious work.[35]

We do not merely have to address a conflict around financial resources ("Your work has become too much of an idol—refocus on the matters of heaven by giving to the new church building fund"), but also a clash around time and service ("You are

---

35   Dorothy Sayers, "Why Work?" *Letters to a Diminished Church*, 1942.

working too much—please resolve this by volunteering with a Wednesday night church program"). Now, for the umpteenth time (and many more times yet to come), *I fervently support Christian tithing and service, and hope all men and women of faith are using their resources of time and treasure in a plethora of ways that advance the Kingdom of God.* I assume some of that takes place within the church and some without, but one's commitments of time, treasure, and service are an important part of one's Christian walk. And the church has every right (and obligation) to preach about that *in the church.*

What I am concerned about is the belief that this message must frame the interests of one's work and vocation as against the interests of the church. It is not only theologically problematic but riddled with conflict, and devoid of the holistic Scriptural coherence that ought to be the church's aim.

My Preemptive Apology

In my preparations for this chapter, I met with a couple dozen pastors who almost universally assured me that their focus was aligned with my message. I believe most of them wholeheartedly. I have not meant to cause offense in this chapter, even if some of my words were harsh. I lovingly suggest that some churches that believe they are teaching a whole-Bible message about work are not and have capitulated to the easier and more palatable message that speaks with suspicion and caution about work, and focuses instead on "generosity" and "ministry service." If I were a pastor, I would want to speak on generosity and service, and I fault no one for doing so. I also fault no pastor for preaching about work by coupling it to messages on the dangers of greed, vanity, and idolatry.

Friends, the message that you of good faith are after is not getting through. Far too many churchgoers simply aren't hearing about work as the purpose of life—as an act of worship to God, the first and ultimate worker. Instead, they're hearing the culturally convenient message that we do the work we have to do to get by, but that our work must never be in the real echelon of our highest ordered priorities—is being heard and believed even if it not being spoken and taught. I plead with those clergy who believe the Bible's whole message on work to preach so unapologetically, giving the audience the takeaway they so desperately need to hear.

To Work Is to Be Human, and to Be Human Is to Work

I benefited tremendously from reading Tim Keller's wonderful book *Every Good Endeavor: Connecting Your Work to God's Work*. I believe the message of the book and the heart behind it are very much compatible with what I am writing in this book (though surely Keller's work is far superior in prose, depth, and Biblical teaching).

I worry too many pastors have read Keller's book but stopped there. They have been unwilling to preach, and I mean preach *regularly*, on the subject. A Christian's relationship to work is not "one and done." The tools needed to appreciate Biblical teaching on work require an ongoing effort that will involve recurring pulpit teaching.

When Keller refers to our work endeavors as rearranging the raw materials of a particular domain to draw out its potential for the flourishing of everyone, he speaks to creational theology. Per Keller, the Biblical language speaks of us as gardeners, taking an active approach to the work we are tasked with. In all domains, occupations, and categories of life, we are gardening—working towards a process of creative and productive activity that is at the heart of why we are here on earth. This is a Biblical message, and it needs to be a recurring Sunday morning message.

I will close this chapter with yet another quote from Dorothy Sayers, who intuitively understood the humanity of work, and, in that context, the God-created humanness of work. If we believe that to work is human and to be human is to work, then surely the church, out of its care for the human person, must find a way to better teach this message.

> *If work is to find its right place in the world, it is the duty of the Church to see to it that the work serves God, and that the worker serves the work.*[36]

---

36   Ibid.

MONEY AND AMBITION

IDOLS OR HEALTHY MOTIVATORS?

TO-GOS AT TOGO'S SANDWICH

The spirit of commerce brings with it the spirit of frugality, of economy, of moderation, of work, of wisdom, of tranquility, of order, and of regularity.

—Charles de Montesquieu

No society can surely be flourishing and happy, of which the far greater part of the members are poor and miserable.

—Adam Smith

I closed out my prior chapter with some kind words about Pastor Tim Keller's wonderful book *Every Good Endeavor*. I meant what I said. I believe it to be a theologically astute treatment of the way God views our work, and it captured a far larger audience than this book will surely reach. I believe an approach to work rooted in creational theology and the dignity of the human person is desperately needed in a time when most pro-work books are rooted in some form of weak utilitarianism.

The Missing Endeavor

Keller's book does immeasurable good in establishing the creative and dignifying aspects of work. On a practical basis, though, the book—likely by design—largely avoids the subject of money and economics. Even the second part of the book, dedicated to problems with work, focuses on potential fruitless-ness and pointlessness, not monetary considerations. Warnings against selfishness focus on vanity and status, not financial aspi-ration. Pastor Keller has written multiple works decrying the idolatry of money,[37] and no one is likely confused as to where he stands in this regard. I would suggest that for a book to deal comprehensively with a Christian's attitude, approach, and behavior concerning work, some discussion of career ambition, including financial ramifications, is needed.

It is valid and necessary to make a case for hard work as ther-apeutic for the human soul, and I have hopefully done that in chapter 1 of this work. Demonstrating that God created us to work as His image-bearers is foundational, and I hope chapter 3 of this book makes that case. Yet, it is fair to ask, "Is finan-cial well-being an acceptable motivator in how we approach our work lives?" A holistic understanding of work must integrate the practical and financial with the theological and spiritual. That will be the aim of this chapter.

The Debate That Never Ends

What I can't do in this chapter is relitigate the basic case for wealth or prosperity. I will have to touch on this as I argue that working for financial improvement is acceptable, but I will mostly focus on where ambition and work intersect, not the

---

37   Timothy Keller, *Counterfeit Gods: The Empty Promises of Money, Sex, and Power, and the Only Hope That Matters*, Penguin Books, 2011.

broader ethical treatment of riches in the life of a Christian. I certainly am not arrogant enough to think that I could resolve that debate in this chapter, and I long ago accepted that the tensions Christians feel around this subject are both healthy and permanent.

The Bible has 2,350 verses dealing with the subject of money. Eleven of the forty parables Jesus told dealt with money. As money appears in Scriptural texts more often than the subjects of faith or prayer do, it is clear that a Christian's relationship to money is important to God. The debate I refer to as "unsolvable" is not about whether or not the Bible speaks on the subject of money. It self-evidently does.

The tension centers on the fact that the Bible presents wealth as a blessing and a reward for diligent work, and yet warns repeatedly against idolizing riches. I have been engaged with this subject intellectually, spiritually, and professionally my entire adult life and am convinced that very few people are comfortable holding this tension in place. I am equally convinced, though, that that is exactly what we are supposed to do. It might be easier to decide we like one Scriptural teaching and will disregard another, but this isn't a great option for a Bible-believing Christian. The tension embedded here is not paradoxical and does not force us to pick sides between competing Bible verses—it simply requires us to hold in tension truths that present challenge, complexity, and a need for wisdom.

Riches for Me but Not for Thee

The way in which most Christians deal with this tension is difficult to describe without offending some (perhaps many) people. The offense will not come from the delivery, as this presentation is meant to be charitable and civil. Rather, the offense comes in the case being made itself, as countless people hear the description and think, "Oh, I think he is talking about me." I can understand why a lot of people think it may be describing them—it is elucidating a widespread, systemic mentality.

To what am I referring, exactly? The most common way that people deal with the tension between Biblical support for wealth and its warnings against idolatry and greed. The kneejerk response is to accumulate the amount of money needed to sustain their own comforts, convenience, and peace, then immediately view anyone above that line as in a moral violation of excess. In other words, we find a lifestyle that is attainable and comfortable, then proceed to judge those who have more. We see this as a perfect solution—it provides people their desired material comforts and amenities, while allowing them the sanctimonious moral superiority complex that always accompanies envy.

I am well aware that not everyone does this consciously. I do not believe that judgment against those of various financial positions is always explicit. I am referring to an underlying mentality that rationalizes a certain quality of life (a quality of life, I would add, that shouldn't need rationalization), and yet acts as if the "danger zone" of Biblical warning about wealth begins right above their line and position. Candidly, it is exhausting.

But it is also incredibly human. We are not hardwired with great self-awareness. It's unfortunate, but understandable. I simply want readers to be aware of it and recognize it for what it is—a moral position born of convenience.

In Newport Beach, California, where I have spent most of my adult life, there is a tendency in evangelicalism to evaluate one's financial situation for its moral context relative only to others in Newport Beach, without considering the rest of the world. Well-meaning (sometimes) Christians who live in $2 million homes (a modest home value in Newport Beach), surrounded by comforts that 99.9 percent of the world would not even be able to comprehend tell themselves that they are "middle class" and "opposed to extravagance." They get their house payment covered (or mortgage paid off). They settle on certain vacations, cars, and outings that are nowhere near the most extravagant in an affluent city like Newport Beach. Feeling assured of their own security and well-being, they dare to feel that they are somehow in the middle of the road economically, as if the rest of the world did not exist.

Clean-Up in Aisle Sanctimony

I do not believe the lifestyle of those predicating their moral judgments about wealth and prosperity on their own achievement of certain comfort and security is remotely unbiblical. My critique is not of how people of various socioeconomic positions live, per se, but rather of the never-ending quest to seek moral superiority by placing oneself below a certain level, without considering the tiers of economic positions beneath them. A greater self-awareness would force the person I am describing to answer the two questions that they have gone to great subconscious lengths to make sure they never have to address:

1. Is the position I am in morally acceptable?
2. Is the position those who have more than me are in morally acceptable?

Examining these two questions in concert causes us to realize that 99 percent of the time our feelings about number 2 are driven by covetousness, not an absolute standard of morally acceptable wealth. But we are not going to let ourselves say, without qualification, that financial accumulation is acceptable. It feels too greedy, too worldly, too uncomfortable. That said, we certainly aren't going to go without the degree of peace and security that we enjoy. Therefore, we create the moral distinction necessary for us to have our cake and eat it too. We condemn extravagance and opulence without specificity. We critique those who own a boat (as long as we don't have one), other than when they invite us to join them for an afternoon on it. We speak publicly and often about the vacations we can't afford, but never about the vacations we do take.

We do whatever mental gymnastics are necessary to tell ourselves that we are not "that guy" (the richer one), then use that to justify our own economic position, which may not be quite as impoverished and challenged as we think.

Biblical Clarity

The tension over the rewards and perils of wealth cannot be resolved through self-delusion and mental gymnastics. Both sides must be held in balance, recognizing the full and beautiful truth in all Biblical revelation. And this is to be done not because it makes us feel better about ourselves, but because it honors the whole counsel of God.

The Bible really does commend the diligent hands that generate wealth (Prov. 10:4). It really does commend saving for nice things (Prov. 21:20). It really does speak of wealth as a blessing (Prov. 10:22). It identifies God as the source of our ability to create wealth (Deut. 8:18) and encourages us to ask him for greater prosperity (I Chron. 4:10). It establishes the reward of profit as the just result of hard work (Prov. 14:23).

And that same Bible commands us to be generous (Prov. 22:9). It demands that we not boast in our riches (Jer. 9:23) or put our hope in them (I Tim. 6:17). It condemns greed (Col. 3:5) and reminds us that we can only serve one master (Matt. 6:24).

It decries the love of money (Heb. 13:5). It teaches a lifestyle of generosity (Luke 10:30–37) and reminds us that everything belongs to the Lord (Ps. 24:1).

Hundreds of verses demonstrate that the Bible speaks positively of financial incentives, and hundreds of proof texts are available warning against an idolatrous attachment to one's worldly possessions. The duty of the Christian is to recognize the sinful allure of extremes on both sides of the scale—repudiating ambition on one side and idolizing the accumulation of money on the other. Understanding these passages and the broader topic requires a commitment to Biblical wisdom and a recognition that what is at stake is really our hearts. Always and forever, the Bible speaks to the state of our hearts, rather than decreeing an exactly maximum dollar amount.

A heart of generosity does not seek recognition for generosity, and it does not keep score. A heart opposed to idolatry doesn't succumb to the temptation to believe that we are the master of our own fates. It feels daily gratitude for the Lord's provision. The Christian heart seeks a Biblical integration of these concepts without concern for how it makes us feel or look.

If there's one word I think encapsulates the modern church's processing of these concepts it is "Phariseeism." We are so uncomfortable admitting that we want our own creature comforts that we manufacture ways to pharisaically pretend otherwise. We live in the "relative" (how much better others are doing than us) rather than the "absolute" (how well we are doing). We never stop to consider that our entire engagement with this topic is rooted in our desire for a certain minimum quality of life. We tell others how they ought to be, not realizing that we ourselves haven't reconciled the Biblical tension on the subject.

Corner Office

So, what is the line when it comes to vocational ambition? Is a Christian permitted to make career decisions motivated by their own material well-being, or does that go against the moral imperative to live a life of productivity, innovation, and creativity? Does our promotion of work end with the teleological or does it extend to the economic? If some concern over prosperity is called for, where do we draw the line?

I call this the "corner-office" dilemma—should a worker who is doing well, who has a nice office and is appropriately recognized, be content there? Or is it acceptable to press harder in pursuit of greater achievement and success? Is the corner office a permissible goal for a Christian professional?

The tension when we apply economic cost-benefits to the workforce is not any different than the aforementioned tension between the Bible's teachings on wealth. We reconcile ourselves to this balancing act. Is it wrong for a Christian to desire a raise, a larger bonus, and a higher position with the company? Of course not. I can make an argument that in some cases it is wrong not to! But should that desire become an obsession, an idol, and an excuse for sin and neglect? Again, of course not. The Bible doesn't tell us an exact maximum level of output that is allowed. We are not told a salary at which our aspirations for more must end.

We know there is a minimum level of financial consideration that is not just allowed but required. Basic responsibility demands we live up to our obligations, save diligently, care for our families, and exercise responsible stewardship. We also know there comes a point at the other end of the scale that may very well cause us to ignore our families, fail in relational duties, undermine our responsibilities as a spouse or parent, and even fall prey to the worship of mammon.

The Hard Truth

There is a spot between where financial responsibility is honored and financial idolatry is avoided. That spot is not an exact income level, house size, or 401(k) balance. It is an individual effort to integrate calling, dreams, aspirations, and responsibilities in a way that follows God's counsel. It is not defined by a pastor because there is not a verse that quantifies it. It is a byproduct of soul-searching and rightly ordered love. It is different for each person because each person was created individually.

This is perhaps one of the most pressing things I want to communicate in this book. Recognizing that God made us all differently, with different passions and interests, has profound implications for our lives and careers. That realization is also relevant to the topic of where financial matters fit into one's work habits and decisions.

Does every artist need to drill deep into the commercial implications of their artwork, provided their basic financial responsibilities are met? Of course not. Does every entrepreneur need to check out at 5:00 p.m. every evening to make sure they never miss a family meal? Certainly not. Some lines of work afford different flexibilities than others, which extends to financial considerations as well. Our individuality as people created in the image of God brings with it certain universal principles: the dignity of all people, the productive capacity of all people, the need for basic financial responsibility, etc. But we also accept that which is nonuniversal: some people are motivated by experience more than money, some value night school more than overtime pay, and some professions have marginal additional compensation in relation to increased output.

Our individuality means that economic motivators, ramifications, and decision-making are also individual. I am not advocating for ethical relativism. I have drawn two universal lines: one on the side of financial responsibility and stewardship, and the other against greed and idolatry. We should never color between those two lines with the crayons of Phariseeism or covetousness.

We can condemn unequivocally the person who looks down on anyone who seems to sacrifice for the sake of their career, all while celebrating their good fortunes when it benefits the sanctimonious one (the aforementioned afternoon on their boat, a visit to their vacation home, a nice dinner out where they pick up the tab). To revisit the ecclesiastical theme of the last chapter, how often have churches warned the successful entrepreneur against how hard they are working one week, only to ask him or her for a check to the church building fund the next week?

Pick a lane. If someone's diligence, drive, and ambition really bother you, find a way to reconcile that distaste with your worldview (while rooting out possible covetousness). Then, don't seek to benefit from their prosperity on another day. Too many people try to have it both ways.

This is the evangelical dilemma: we want desperately to condemn entrepreneurial and vocational success without losing access to the rewards such success brings with it. This desire to condemn success is what needs to change.

The False Dichotomy of Family vs. Career

I wrote in the introduction of the pop culture zeitgeist surrounding this dichotomy. It would be hard to imagine a more embedded cliché than some person (male or female) who is "too focused on career," who then, courtesy of some plot contrivance (a death in the family, the rekindling of an old romance, a visit to the hometown of their youth, a desire to reunite with an estranged child), learns to abandon the trappings of their career and rediscover the superiority of family, relationships, or love. Perhaps the only time that Hollywood takes a pro-family position these days is when it means condemning careerism.

The advantage of this binary is that no decent person is ever comfortable picking something over their own family. I'm not advocating for people to choose career over marriage or children in these modern movie plots—it is that the two options are presented as mutually exclusive to begin with, and that the foil is always—*always*—one's job.

A refresher on the Biblical warnings of wealth is in order, i.e., the avoidance of idolatry. Is work really the only thing we can turn into a false idol? Can one make an idol of their family, their spouse, a relationship, or their children? One of the great things about Tim Keller's ministry was his realization that "counterfeit gods" came in many shapes and sizes. I am just as willing as the next man to tear up as the emotionally shallow businessman leaves his job to give love a chance in his hometown, but it is categorically false that the only danger we face as adults is over-emphasizing work. Many, many people have neglected their work responsibilities in the name of being a "family man," which is equally unacceptable.

I will try to paint a better picture of "balance" in chapter 10 of this book. In the meantime, the theological point must be that all forms of idolatry are wrong, whether that idol be our financial well-being or our familial relationships.

Warnings are frequently needed when career devotion is getting in the way of family relationships, marriage covenants, and the joys of parenthood. I have rarely met someone who has executed it all flawlessly. What I know from Scripture is that our career goals and financial aspirations need not be pitted against our families. Just as we are to make room in our lives for all sorts of heathy priorities and responsibilities, there is space for earnest professional ambition that leaves us the capacity to care for those we love.

Getting Right What Too Many Get Wrong

A contemporary conception of career development is often rooted in the love of mammon. My worldview does not deny the existence of materialistic tendencies in modern work habits. I know what Gordon Gekko meant in *Wall Street* when he said that "greed is good." I remember the portrayal of the "yuppies" in the show *Thirtysomething*. I am well aware that for many, work ambitions are motivated by the desire for nicer clothes, nicer cars, and nicer vacations.

That is not what I am advocating for.

My theology of work centers on the intersection of our passions and our skills, providing a venue for acting out our God-given capacity for productivity and creativity. I believe that people naturally have varying degrees of measurable financial ambition that goes along with this. In all cases, I hope both Phariseeism and idolatry will be avoided and that a true heart of generosity will be present. I know the world sometimes misses the mark here. Commercialism, materialism, and the pursuit of thoughtless accumulation are all around us. They are not the subject of this chapter.

Through all of the needed warnings found in the tension of Biblical teaching, what I admire is ambition. Indeed, the people most likely to condemn ambition depend on someone having it. The pastors preaching against it need the fruits of that ambition tree. Society requires citizens who exhibit talent, skill, and risk-taking in order to develop the goods and services that enhance the quality of life of those around them. Sometimes people get bonuses and stock options and car allowances and corner offices out of these efforts. Sometimes they find or feel rewards in different ways. It is counterproductive to condemn the pursuit of material reward, especially one best identified in the achievement of some form of comfort or convenience. No one criticizes comfort or convenience until they have secured comfort and convenience themselves, regardless of the hierarchal stratum that represents.

I believe God made us to work, and I think sometimes that comes with the need for economic ambition. I believe some people are less drawn to such material aspirations, but I also know this: when the toil is hard and the work becomes rewarding, blessings often follow. We should not stand in the way of that for anyone.

This is what I have observed to be good: that it is appropriate for a person to eat, to drink and to find satisfaction in their toilsome labor under the sun during the few days of life God has given them—for this is their lot. Moreover, when God gives someone wealth and possessions, and the ability to enjoy them, to accept their lot and be happy in their toil—this is a gift of God.

—Ecclesiastes 5:18-19 (NIV)

THE ECONOMIC CASE

CASE

WE PRODUCE, THEREFORE WE ARE

INSIDE SALES REP AT MUSIC COMPANY

Every individual, from the common mechanic, that works in wood or clay, to the prime minister that regulates with the dash of his pen the agriculture, the breeding of cattle, the mining, or the commerce of a nation, will perform his business the better, the better he understands the nature of things, and the more his understanding is enlightened.

—*Jean-Baptiste Say*

Produce, produce! Were it but the pitifulest, infinitesimal fraction of a product, produce it in God's name. 'Tis the utmost thou hast in thee? Out with it then! Up, up! Whatsoever thy hand findeth to do, do it with thy whole might.

—*Thomas Carlyle*

I am convinced that one of the greatest sources of a low view of work is a misunderstanding of economics. I do not mean a *lack* of understanding but, rather, a *flawed* understanding. Too many people not only lack a true comprehension of how human action works, but also believe something about our activity that is fundamentally false. The famous line often attributed to Mark Twain comes to mind:

> *It ain't what you don't know that gets you into trouble*
> *It's what you know for sure that just ain't so.*

Two Competing Economic Visions

While our political divisions may indicate that the great economic disagreement we face is the size and scope of government, I am convinced that the fundamental divide between the two primary economic camps today is not "big government versus small government." This can lead to the classic debate of "central planning versus laissez-faire," but at its root, this is a debate over the primacy of *production* versus *consumption*.

To be clear, I strongly suspect one's verdict in the production versus consumption debate will heavily influence one's vision for the size of government and opinion on the merits and limits of central planning. However, the underlying divide is based on what one understands the sine qua non (the essential essence) of economic activity to be.

Keeping It Classic: Supply and Demand

The classical economic school is commonly understood as synonymous with a laissez-faire ("leave alone") approach to economic life. In contrast to the feudal, monarchic, and top-down systems prevalent for centuries prior to the Enlightenment, the classical school rejected excessive government interference.

The great moral philosopher Adam Smith, widely considered the father of classical economics, changed the West's understanding of economic life through new theories of self-interest, trade, and prices. While concepts like the "invisible hand," the division of labor, and well-known economic laws like the law of supply and demand are most affiliated with the classical school, it was a lesser-known French economist who distilled classical economic thought into something actionable.

The line *"supply creates its own demand"* is often attributed to Jean-Baptiste Say, although most scholars acknowledge that the exact statement comes from John Maynard Keynes when summarizing the work of Say.[38] The notion of supply creating its own demand is referred to as Say's law, and it serves as the case for a production-focused economy.

Before any of us can be a source of demand, we must first be a source of supply, and what nearly all of us supply is work. Those who want to exchange a product or service for another product or service first had to obtain that product through the fruits of their labor. If it was not from a paycheck but rather from a natural resource they had access to (e.g., fruit from a tree they owned), they still had to add work to the commodity to package the "supply" brought to the transaction. Most often, we sell our labor to entrepreneurs who themselves create an item of value (i.e., we work for an organization that supplies a product or service). The point is the same if we contribute our labor to our own entrepreneurial endeavor. We produce goods and services of value and exchange them for equally valuable goods and services, acting within society's structure of different needs,

---

38 Steven Kates, "'Supply Creates its Own Demand': A Discussion of the Origins of the Phrase and of its Adequacy as an Interpretation of Say's Law of Markets," *History of Economics Review*, Volume 41, Issue 1, 2005.

tastes, and values. Our production creates a market for other goods and services. Rinse and repeat.

What Jean-Baptiste Say taught us is that if we become over-supplied in one product, we must have underproduced another. Prices drop for the overproduced item and rise for the underproduced, incentivizing more production of the scarce product. A robust economy never needs to settle for less output, but rather is always adjusting the "mix." Prices will adjust to incentivize proper production and consumption (lower for less desirable items, higher for more desirable items). Production is always the fuel of this economic engine.

People, of course, may be driven by different motives and incentives in their own productive activity. They may want to consume what someone else produces in exchange for their own output. I cannot make myself a new laptop computer, but I can do financial advisory work that provides me the resources to buy the laptop someone else produced. Even when one wants to save the capital accumulated from productive activity, that capital either becomes a means of future consumption, or it becomes the capital that funds new productive capacity: new inventions, new factories, new business endeavors, etc.

Say's law is an indisputable truth in a macroeconomic sense: the total production of goods and services drives the total demand in an economy. The fundamental challenge of economic life is *production*—that is, creating the incentives and conditions that will maximize productive output.

The Economic Debate of the Century

In the twentieth century, a new school of economic thought framed our economic challenge in a different way. Contra the classical school and its focus on production, Keynesianism—the brainchild of Depression-Era British economist John Maynard Keynes—posits that *consumption* is the primary driver of economic activity. Keynes feared that a drop in consumption (or the appetite for consumption, what Keynes referred to as "animal spirits") could lead to a decline in production that would trigger a negative feedback loop of less hiring, lower wages, decreased consumption, and so on. To Keynes, promoting "aggregate demand" would solve this problem.

Close study of markets shows that, challenges and inevitabilities in the business cycle notwithstanding, a fall in prices also decreases the price of production cost. In a given market, prices drop until they reach a level at which there is a restoration of incentive to produce that raises hiring, wages, and output, and with it, natural consumptive activity. The non-Keynesian never denies that there can be downward pressure on demand; he or she simply suggests that the solution is in market forces (and prices) working themselves out without interventions or distortions that come at a cost. When economic conditions seem troubled, political leaders and central planners will advocate for intervention. In contrast, advocating for self-correcting market mechanisms does not provide more power to politicians or require heavy central planning, so it is less likely that politicians or central planners will call for a hands-off approach.

I would argue that a lot of economic debate could be saved by starting with the theological case—the very case I made in chapter 3. The first flaw of Keynesianism is anthropological. Mankind's created purpose was to drive cultivation, creativity, productivity, and stewardship—i.e., to produce. A laser focus on consumption will gradually erode wealth. Prioritizing our fundamental purpose would have saved Keynes, and with him all of modern economics, from the wild goose chase of demand stimulation. If we already know that God made us to produce, we don't need to spend a century wondering how best to manipulate demand in pursuit of economic growth.

This academic experiment has not gone well. We're now faced with excessive indebtedness around the globe and a universal dependency on government intervention to cancel out economic slowdown in the business cycle.

Human Nature 101

Human beings do not need to be told to want things. We are created with desires, tastes, and appetites that operate independent of economic manipulation or government intervention. We can be incentivized to produce more for the purpose of consuming more, but generating the desire to consume is never the challenge. There are always human needs that remain unmet, therefore, there are no limits on the incentive to produce.

We achieve more wealth in society when we produce more than we consume. This basic tautology (W=P-C) is the backbone of cogent economic thought. Wealth comes from production of goods and services that enhance the quality of life of people in society. Consumption is only limited by our ability to produce, and when we produce more than we consume, we build wealth. Fewer houses, cars, appliances, and technologies does not make us wealthier. Nor does a stronger supply of consumer demand. Wealth is always created by a stronger supply of the goods and services that humans demand. We overcome the burden of scarcity through production. Confusing the supply *of goods and services* and the supply *of demand for these services* has been the cause of nearly endless economic fallacy and chaos over the last seventy-five years.

The modern expression of classical, production-focused economics is called the supply-side movement. When a group of economic intellectuals (including Dr. Art Laffer and Dr. Robert Mundell) and a group of media editorialists (including Robert Bartley and Jude Wanniski) influenced a group of American political leaders (e.g., Jack Kemp and Ronald Reagan) in the late 1970s, this entire ethos found new life in public policy. You might associate these names or the phrase "supply-side movement" only with advocacy for lower taxes, but the underlying philosophy is a belief that production drives economic growth. In a supply-friendly vision of the economy, removing high taxes and burdensome regulations is seen as removing impediments to productive activity.

All political and economic debate aside, the supply-side movement and the classical school of economics are rooted in the belief that economic growth comes from production. This economic view is consistent with the theological view presented in this book: our God-created purpose since the Garden of Eden is production. Work drives purpose, meaning, and wealth in a nation and society.

The Macro to the Micro and Back

These high-level principles are not merely abstractions reserved for our academic understanding of macroeconomics. While the principles of classical economics, including Say's law, stress the primacy of production in driving economic growth across a society, the application to the person (microeconomics) is equally important.

When we speak of a person producing something, we describe how they combine inputs to create an output. This often involves a person combining something material (plastic, steel, rubber) with something immaterial (knowledge, ideas, systems) to create a product or service that is useful to human beings.

At both the macro and micro levels, economics combines the physical and the immaterial. As individuals, we live in a combination of material and spiritual realities, and we do this as creatures made *imago dei*. In other words, we are both physical and spiritual beings ("dust of the ground" *and* "breath of life"). The Christian doctrine of incarnation illuminates Jesus becoming fully man while also being fully God. Christ incarnate took on both the material and spiritual aspects of our humanity. My entire philosophy of economics is rooted in the quest for human flourishing: the material *and* spiritual abundance, peace, joy, and harmony that are the telos of human endeavor. The Gnostic heresy we discussed in prior chapters regards the immaterial or spiritual as superior to the physical or material. Our view of economics sees both as equally important to God, and equally significant in economic practice.

Production is not just a physical matter. It happens only when one combines physical material or activity with mental exertion. We combine knowledge, ideas, and experimentation with physical materials to create output. This is the production process, and it drives a market economy. Land, labor, and capital are the key factors in macroeconomic production, but nonphysical elements like entrepreneurship and technology become key components at a micro level. Commodities and materials are vital, but so is the human being's immaterial contribution. Each person works on a micro level within production factors at a macro level that help inputs drive improved outputs—the micro and macro, married together.

Without This, Nothing

There is no production without the meeting of a human need. The satisfaction of human wants and needs is the reason for productive activity. We measure productive success by the satisfaction it brings those served by the goods and services produced. That satisfaction can be measured in the income produced: the real output minus the real input. If a customer will pay $100 for something that cost $50 to produce, there is a profit (income). If the customer will pay $40 for that which cost $50 to produce, there is a loss—satisfaction for the customer is beneath the level needed to incentivize production. We can focus on lowering input costs, contributing additional input from ideas and technology, but ultimately the output will determine if there is income or loss. That output is essentially a measurement of human satisfaction.

This is not merely a mathematical formula. As an economist, I see measurements of production as important. But underlying the equations and ratios is human endeavor—the utility we bring human beings through the goods or services we produce.

The Dignity of Productive Work throughout History

Intellectual and spiritual leaders have opined across millennia on the nature of productive work.

Aristotle distinguished between *poiesis* (activities designed to produce an outcome) and *praxis* (activities done for their own sake).[39]

The early church father Saint Augustine provided revolutionary insight on the ways that productive work is inherently dignified and vital to our well-being.[40]

---

39   Oded Balaban, "Praxis and Poesis in Aristotle's Practical Philosophy," *The Journal of Value Inquiry*, July 1990.

40   Dr. Megan DeVore, "The Labors of our Occupation: Can Augustine Offer Any Insight on Vocation?" *The Southern Baptist Journal of Theology*, Volume 22, Unit 1, 2018.

Saint Thomas Aquinas provided church tradition an authoritative case for productive work, tied to the dignity of the human person and part of the case for private property.[41]

Adam Smith demonstrated that the unleashed productivity of a division of labor simultaneously creates specialization in our work and greater access to a range of goods and services.[42]

As mentioned earlier in this chapter, Jean-Baptiste Say built a foundation for the idea that production is the macroeconomic catalyst of all economic activity.

Max Weber theorized that the Calvinist ethic of engaging with what was previously considered secular work became the root of modern capitalism, dignifying productive activity as serving the common good. In Weber's work, we see historical connective tissue between Reformation theology's emphasis on productivity and the significant economic progress of the next few centuries.[43]

The late 1970s saw a renewed commitment to Say's law and the primacy of economic incentives for productivity in media, academia, and, most importantly, public policy as the supply-side movement gathered both political and popular appeal.[44] Removing impediments to producing goods and services became a fundamental plank in the platform of the Republican Party and influenced the thinking of many Americans.

---

41 *Summa Theologica*, Part I–II, Q66, Answers 1–2; and, Marc Vincent Rugani, "St. Thomas Aquinas on the Goodness and Right to Work Today," October 2018.

42 Adam Smith, *The Wealth of Nations, Book 1, Chapter One: On the Division of Labour*, 1776.

43 Max Weber, *The Protestant Ethic and the Spirit of Democratic Capitalism*, 1905.

44 Brian Domitrovic, *Econoclasts: The Rebels Who Sparked the Supply-Side Revolution and Restored American Prosperity*, ISI, 2009.

Now, Keynesianism has become the market gospel, rooted in a deep distrust of markets and their ability to self-correct over time. The Keynesian ideology, contrary to the giants who came before him, seeks the aid of the federal government in stimulating aggregate demand, calling on central planners to steward the affairs of the economy rather than rely on incentives for productivity. This Keynesian mantra has never been confined to the role of a counter-cyclical fiscal boost in times of economic slowdown. It treats mankind as a consumer that needs to be told to demand goods and services during times of muted appetite. Keynesianism fails to see mankind's true nature. Its unrelenting focus on consumption has allowed a declining view of work and productivity to permeate modern economics, particularly in public policy.

This tragic misapprehension of the role of productive activity has spread beyond the halls of power into the culture at large. The notion of production as primary to consumption has been excised from our thinking, and the fundamental truth that all production must serve another human being has been lost—economically and otherwise.

Keynesian fallacies have impacted government, pop culture, the church, and more. Our prima facie policy response to economic challenges now is to hope that we can inspire people to shop. Consumer spending and consumer confidence dominate economic metrics. Worst of all, the culture has fully lost its appreciation for service—and who is served—in our work.

Working for Good for Humans

Having retired from hosting late-night talk shows for over three decades, comedian David Letterman began hosting a show on Netflix a few years ago where he converses with prominent celebrities and public figures. In an episode with comedian Jerry Seinfeld, Letterman expresses regret for staying in the late-night television business for so long. Notice the reasoning Letterman offers for this self-critical regret:

> I should've left ten years ago, because then I could've taken some of that energy and focus and applied it to actually doing something good for humans.[45]

In fairness to Letterman's guest, Seinfeld did not let the inherent error in Letterman's thinking go uncorrected:

> The people that are good at it do it because they know it's making people happy, and that's what's driving them, and that's why you were so great.

The reproach Letterman gave his own career is rooted in the mistaken belief that his own productive effort was only about him, not the people he was serving. I do not know what other talents or gifts David Letterman may have, but I imagine he would be hard-pressed to find something he does better than make people laugh, especially in the competitive venue of late-night television. If "doing good for humans" was the goal, he did it and then some.

The idea of taking "energy and focus and applying it elsewhere," misses the virtue in what he was already doing to serve humans: *it could only have been done because it was serving human beings*. Because Letterman was compensated well for his rare talent, perhaps he feels guilty. But, as Seinfeld pointed out, he is expressing regret for "making people happy." This is not something for which we should feel guilt—this is productive work.

---

45 *My Next Guest Needs No Introduction*, Netflix, May 8, 2018.

Not all of us are late-night comedians or "make people happy" with the output of our work. But we might also be guilty of thinking that our work is not noble or for the greater good. Christians often use the term "tentmaking" to describe an act of commerce supplementing the ministerial work of a pastor. This expression comes from the fact that Paul the Apostle worked as a tentmaker when congregations could not support him financially (Acts 18:1–4). Either through implicit or explicit error, this expression has become a euphemism for "second-tier work"—a "necessary evil" done purely for transactional or pragmatic reasons that is less worthy than "elevated" pastoral work.

Tentmaking meets human needs, or else it would not offer any financial compensation at all. It is the productive combination of inputs (skills and materials) towards an output that meets a human need. Paul himself described tentmaking as hard work that meets the needs of others, while giving him the resources for his own needs to be met (Acts 20:33–35).

This bi-vocational language, often used to separate professional ministry efforts from moneymaking efforts, is dualist, offensive, and possibly Gnostic. In other words, it overlooks the dignity of our fundamental human purpose: to work. In the marketplace, we meet human needs through the production of goods and services.

Consumption is second to production in an economy because without my own productive activity, I cannot consume; and without someone else's productive activity, there would be nothing for me to consume. A focus on productive work not only builds income, profits, and formulaic measures like GDP, but it restores a sense of service to others in our labor.

Imagining a life of consumption divorced from production is not just spiritually and theologically misguided, it is economically incoherent.

We produce because we exist. Our human appetites and desires always lead to consumption, but our consumption can only follow our production and the production of others. Work builds personal and national wealth and offers the goods and services that enhance the quality of our lives.

RETIREMENT
DISASTER

RETHINKING THE IDEA OF A
THIRTY-YEAR VACATION

BOOKING AGENCY & BAND MANAGEMENT FIRM

Half our life is spent trying to find something to do with the time we have rushed through life trying to save.

—Will Rogers

Work is not, primarily, a thing one does to live, but the thing one lives to do. It is, or it should be, the full expression of the worker's faculties, the thing in which he finds spiritual, mental, and bodily satisfaction, and the medium in which he offers himself to God.

—Dorothy Sayers

I have a very strong hunch that this is going to be the chapter most in danger of being misinterpreted or misrepresented, but I am determined to head that off at the pass. Hear me out as I try to make, first, the case for what retirement *should not be*, then add an affirmative case for a healthy and productive vision of retirement.

The argument I make in this chapter is not about *financial freedom*, a concept I very much support. Nor do I think that a steelworker should still be putting on the uniform at seventy-five. I am not arguing against a worker leaving the job at which they spent the bulk of their career—well, not *always* against it. I do not suggest that the same stress and exertion one experiences at age thirty-five ought to be present at seventy.

Nor should this chapter be read as just offering the accepted bromides about retirement—one that supplements the vision of a "thirty-year vacation" with various platitudes around "giving back," "volunteering," or other forms of activity that are meant to substitute for real exertion. I can respect the fact that proponents of the anti-work vision for retirement felt the need to amend their multi-decade marketing plan to include imagery of senior citizens doing just enough to check a box of self-realization or modern purpose.

That doesn't cut it.

I do not want to be another critic seeking to tear down with nothing to build up in replacement—which is where my proactive case comes in. But before we can get there, we must assess where we are and how our society got to be this way.

The Problem with What We're Being Sold

If public posturing and marketing campaigns are to be believed, the modern purpose of work can be defined thus: *"Work is what you do so that eventually you won't have to do it anymore."*

No, thank you.

The underlying message of all financial services messaging—of billions of dollars of print, television, and internet advertising, and of the entire model of careerism established in modern life—is that *one works for the purpose of accumulating the capital that will then afford one the ability not to have to work anymore.* Yearning for a post-work life is illustrated in marketing campaigns showing people lounging on a yacht, playing with grandkids in a lake house, traveling, and generally enjoying their freedom from a life glued to a desk or trapped in an office.

The difference in visuals in this advertising for retirement versus general tourism is only the age of the people featured in the ads. Ads depicting a twenty-nine-year-old enjoying a cruise vacation and a sixty-five-year-old in a retirement home are essentially interchangeable.

Few elements of American life are more deeply seated in our subconscious than the image of a clean break from our careers, followed by living out our golden years outside of the confines of work, office, factory, classroom, or whatever vocational venue. It is rooted in the idea that what stands between you and a thirty-year vacation is only one thing: "a number." Achieve the (financial) number you need that will last you the rest of your life. Plan for inflation, taxes, second homes, support for aging parents, support for young-adult children, and market returns. From there, a life of leisure, peace, relaxation, and freedom supposedly awaits.

State Farm Insurance famously ran a campaign where a worker put in their "fifteen-years notice"—a clever way of showing that workers needed to start planning for their grand exit. Merrill Lynch once ran a campaign showing a six-year-old dreaming of future retirement as Billy Joel's iconic song "My Life" played. Who knew someone who hadn't even started school, let alone work, was already dreaming of the day they would no longer have to work? Charles Schwab's 2010 self-mocking campaign featured a man in his early sixties wondering why his financial advisor was talking to him about buying a vineyard.[46] The man in the commercial didn't want the cliché of a beach house or vineyard—he wanted someone to tell him the bottom-line numbers and plan that he needed to know he was done.

Not all advertisements are equally absurd, but all are seemingly rooted in the same assumption: people's universal financial goal is not to work. Short-term goals like buying a house and intermediate goals like funding college for one's kids are generally included, but the big one is "retirement." An exit. An escape. A departure from drudgery for what looks an awful lot like a vacation.

We can be critical of some ads. I never understood what a humpback whale breaching in the middle of the ocean had to do with a person retiring (Pacific Life Insurance). An orange squirrel bouncing around a house while a middle-aged couple plans various expenditures is not all that appealing to me (Voya Financial). Regardless of subjective thematic or aesthetic decisions of advertisers, it is the objective assertion that what people ought to work for is an accumulated sum of capital that will afford them two, three, or even four decades outside of the workforce. It is a systemic—and grotesque—assumption in financial services and our culture. Here's the problem with what we are being sold.

The Great Enrichment

It has to be said how new this is in all of human history. The life expectancy in the United States was between ages forty and fifty from the end of the Civil War in 1865 until the turn of the

---

46   "Charles Schwab—'Vineyard,'" Havas New York, 2010.

century in 1900. It climbed from fifty to seventy between the beginning of the twentieth century and 1960. A median mortality age of seventy opened up a world of opportunity on Madison Avenue, as national marketers saw a paradigm shift coming in the possibilities of "life after work." The subsequent increase from age seventy to nearly eighty in life expectancy (1960 to present) has put this post-war cultural dynamic on steroids.

The very word "retirement" is a byproduct of two phenomena in the twentieth century that would be foreign to those in the millennia before:

1. The material prosperity sufficient to provide a livelihood apart from work that could span multiple decades.

2. Mortality changes that gave people the option to be out of the workforce for extended parts of their life.

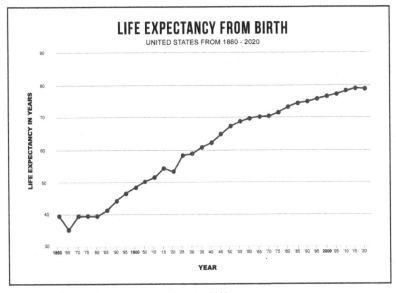

Statista, 2023

A cruder way to put it is that for most of human history, one's retirement plan was, well, to die. The miracle of "the Great Enrichment"[47] is that the vast majority of the human race now lives at a higher quality of life with less physical exertion and toil for a longer and healthier period of time than ever before. From cleaner sanitation and access to food and healthier water supply to protection against natural disasters and vastly improved medical care, we have greatly expanded our quality and quantity of life.

This is, of course, an immeasurable blessing. It is a freedom for which we should live in gratitude. Longer mortalities and healthier loved ones with greater economic resources are all blessings, and my primary concern is how we respond to this development, not the development itself.

I suspect my zeal on this issue would be different if there were a better awareness of the historic novelty of planning for decades of our lives to be spent in leisure and recreation. Starting consideration of what the last decades of our lives are supposed to be with gratitude for the freedom and options we have would be invaluable. The "race to our number" embedded in the marketing messaging of financial services treats retirement like a birthright, not the historically unconventional innovation that it is. When the mental construct is set up as obligation, accountability, constraints, and a demanding boss *versus* a life of freedom, autonomy, vacation, and travel, it's understandable that one's

---

47 The term coined by economist Deirdre McCloskey to describe the 3,000 percent increase in real income per person that started at the beginning of the nineteenth century and has lasted over two centuries. This miraculous period is often said to be the byproduct of liberalized markets that took place after the Enlightenment in concert with a division of labor, more robust access to capital, and, most important, widespread belief in and practice of liberalism. For a greater treatment on the role of human liberty in causing the Great Enrichment: Deirdre McCloskey, "Liberalism Caused the Great Enrichment," University of Chicago, March 31, 2021.

focus gets (falsely) bifurcated. Gratitude for historical context would go a long way in correcting that.

That lack of gratitude has seemingly led to greater perception of drudgery at work, as well as more and more people who view the last ten years (or more) of their career with resentment. There is no reason to believe that the idea that "we work to not work" can be expected to stay limited to the mentality of the eldest age group. The marketing message I critique may be mostly limited to certain assumptions—for example, that most people will be in their late fifties or early sixties before they can afford the "luxury" of a retirement escape—but that doesn't mean the mentality will stay limited to this demographic restraint. After twenty years of watching commercials about "hitting a number" and "leaving the office behind," a thirty-year-old who hits "their number" can be excused for believing that this is what they are supposed to be aiming for as well, even if the stars of those commercials are grandparent-aged adults walking along a beach. After all, it is not their fault that they hit the number early. The aim was a life of leisure and vocational disconnection, right?

Sure, the math of compounding and accumulating sufficient assets leaves many unable to approach their number until age sixty, but that is nowhere near as true as it used to be. Company stock options on Silicon Valley and any other number of "liquidity events" multiply opportunities to hit the number. We bemoan "trust fund babies," young adults who might avoid a job or career because of the financial freedom an inheritance provides. But isn't that same issue at play for a young person who *achieves* financial freedom versus *inheriting* it? Is our concern with trust fund babies only the means by which they received the funds that allowed them a life of inactivity, and not the life of inactivity itself? Shouldn't we hope that a thirty-year-old who has achieved great prosperity early in life (even separate from inheritance) can still live a life of productive activity? Or have they "peaked" at age thirty just because they "hit a number"?

It's unacceptable to think that the dignity of a financially comfortable young adult and their expectations of productivity, creativity, innovation, and service get set to zero because of the balance in their checking account. Never mind the fact that someone who achieves stock option or business sale success at such a young age is highly likely to have a lot more to offer the world in terms of their own entrepreneurial potential.

There is no question that the mentality that leads to greater desire for early departure from the workforce also drives our vision for "retirement" of older men and women. The cultural attitude that "work is what we do to not have to do it anymore" is at the heart of the problem.

The Problem with What We're Being Robbed Of

The oft-ignored problem with our present vision of retirement is that it cuts us off from the productive capacity of talented and experienced people. "Retirement" removes an individual from economic production and replaces it with golf, pickleball, and bridge. This is a form of economic robbery with two victims: the worker with more to add, and the society not receiving their contributions. We are robbed of what individuals have to offer our businesses, stores, plants, factories, and classrooms. The workers themselves are robbed of ongoing productive contribution and the soul-filling benefits that come with such labor. Obviously, each individual situation will be different, and I would not presume to dictate a normative decree of what each company or worker should do. But within the flexibilities that the Great Enrichment has offered us, I would suggest that we are worse off for celebrating our most seasoned, experienced workers and producers being cut off from work and production.

In addition to actual productive work being lost, there is a loss of mentorship that is catastrophic for the well-being of our marketplace. Whether the venue be an office, city hall, school, theater, assembly line, boardroom, or design studio, talented workers in their twenties and thirties benefit immensely from the mentorship of those with twenty or thirty more years of experience. This experience cannot be taught in an employee manual or company video. Many in the first decade or two of their careers might be too shy or too arrogant to seek out mentorship, and many in the final decade or two of this stage of life might be too humble or hesitant to offer themselves up as a mentor. Yet the presence of such experienced workers alongside those newer and younger creates a natural opportunity for mentorship.

I understand there is a need to replace positions over time and finite capacity for workers and roles in various organizations and institutions. The nitty-gritty of how this is accomplished is not what I'm focused on. Rather, I am making the high-level point that rushing our sixty-year-olds out the door is harming our thirty-year-olds.

I am not suggesting that a sixty-five-year-old who has spent forty years at a given company should stay connected to that company forever (though after forty years, perhaps it would be a good place to offer ongoing wisdom and service in one's senior years). I am also not saying that someone who has a really challenging set of circumstances (perhaps bad chemistry with coworkers) needs to remain tethered. I am not suggesting that an NBA player try to make a team when he is fifty, nor am I demanding that a construction worker ache and break their body into their sixties. Each person, and each situation, will call for a different manifestation of what this means.

I am also not intimating that a period of relaxed effort relative to the intensity of "prime" working years is inappropriate. With greater financial freedom comes greater flexibility, and I am not being so draconian as to suggest that the mere aspiration of greater freedom, leisure, and recreation later in life is wrong. That is not what this chapter has been about.

What I am suggesting is that the underlying view that work is something we do in order not to do it anymore is wrong, and that retirement defined as several decades of vacation is unwise and ill-advised.

Retirement vs. Financial Freedom: Purpose and Service

I believe people's self-worth, earned success, sense of purpose, and created capacity for productivity extends into their sixties and seventies. Some form of productive activity is still feasible in the later years of one's life, *even if finances do not require it.*

A variety of venues would benefit from the experience, work, and wisdom of older workers, and banishing them to the golf course, the couch, or even a charity's quarterly board meeting does not maximize the potential and opportunity I am envisioning.

"Retirement" (as defined by our current culture) and financial freedom are not the same thing, conceptually, actionably, or theologically. If one reads this chapter as a critique of "not finan-cially needing to work," they have entirely missed the point. I fully support the efforts of our financial services industry to offer planning and solutions geared towards people achieving financial freedom. I not only support it; I participate in it daily.

I distinguish between the freedom to *do more* financially and the freedom to *do nothing*, because they are entirely different. Yes, one with great (or even adequate) financial resources may be able to keep working and investing, serve on boards, serve at nonprofits, advise entrepreneurs, do consulting, stay in the corner office, work but with limited hours, or any number of other things. Hopefully they take great trips with their grandkids, enjoy the holidays, celebrate anniversaries with even longer trips and sunsets, and get in a few extra rounds of golf. Their financial resources afford them these things, most often as the fruit of a lot of labor and planning.

But that is not the same as working to have the financial freedom to participate in nothing but recreation or leisure. As we think about retirement, we must distinguish between inactivity and financial freedom and attach purpose and service to what we advocate and practice.

The key takeaway of this chapter is that we should rid ourselves of a view of retirement centered on inactivity, and lean into a vision of service, engagement, and activity. These activities will evolve over the course of time, no doubt. The context of one's life and career will create different options and considerations for different people. But a view of service that transcends the token and nominal volunteer seat is the need of the hour.

I humbly suggest that many entrepreneurs who enjoyed a liquidity exit can be more valuable in another entrepreneurial role than they can as a board member at a nonprofit. What one did with one's time, treasure, and talents during their career might be the best place to start when one thinks about the best venue for continued service.

Ken Langone, the multibillionaire cofounder of Home Depot, has his name on numerous hospital buildings in New York City. He has been on the board of the New York Stock Exchange and countless other corporations and charities and has been a frequent media guest. He is a force of nature, and when I first met him, he was seventy-five years old (and yes, already a multibillionaire). He talked about putting his suit and tie on each day to do what he loves doing. Raising money for the St. Patrick's Cathedral renovation, supporting various political candidates, building new businesses, writing a book, investing in new projects—each day is an opportunity to wake up and work. As he put it to me, he has more to do, and feels no need to slow down. At the time of this writing, he is now eighty-seven, and still suiting up.

I seriously doubt that I will be as glued to my computer screen in my seventies as I am now. My calling involves the stewardship of capital on behalf of clients, and I imagine a time will come when I rely more on the portfolio management abilities of others on my team than my own, and my time in front of a screen will be less market-determined. I do a lot of speaking and writing now, but it is limited by the time constraints of the market, of running a complex business, and of serving clients. Perhaps a time will come when there will be more space for speaking and writing—I don't really know.

But I do know that regardless of the precise activity, I cannot imagine my life (and do not want to) without some productive activity. I can see less rigid office hours in the future, and I certainly pray that someday there will be less "tyranny of the inbox" than there is now. Greater freedom for various extracurricular activities sounds lovely, and if I can ever do a vacation without monitoring emails and market interruptions, I will be thrilled. I don't feel in a rush for any of this to change, but I do not foresee any of these things evolving inconsistently with what I have laid out in this chapter. I have the financial freedom to exit the workforce now but find the idea of exiting the business my wife and I have built to be outrageous.

"Retirement" will happen when God takes me to Him. I don't know the day or hour when that will happen, but I do know the kind of life God wants for me until then. While the exact schedule, parameters, daily obligations, and routines will adjust over time—and, Lord willing, time and space for various other activities will open up—I believe that God wants me and that I owe the world around me to stay engaged, hungry, and productive.

The contemporary approach to "retirement" is not merely damaging society as a whole but damaging both those whose contributions are being cut off, and the people who are losing the valuable contributions of those exiting the workforce. It is a lose-lose-lose proposition.

I am not longing for the time when everyone's retirement plan was basically to die! I am tremendously grateful for the greater freedom and flexibility we have now because of improved mortality and economic resources. I find the idea of working less in one's later years as mind and body so require to be perfectly reasonable, even as I hope the wisdom and experience of our senior workforce will not be lost.

May we never equate financial freedom with an exit from those activities that serve others. Productive activity not only stirs our own souls—and minds and bodies—but it blesses the world around us far more than a thirty-year vacation ever could.

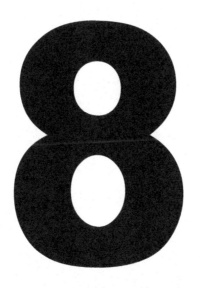

MOVING FROM HALFTIME TO FULL-TIME

SUCCESS AND SIGNIFICANCE ARE NOT AT ODDS

FINANCIAL ADVISOR AT UBS PAINEWEBBER

In nothing has the Church so lost Her hold on reality as in Her failure to understand and respect the secular vocation. She has allowed work and religion to become separate departments, and is astonished to find that, as a result, the secular work of the world is turned to purely selfish and destructive ends, and that the greater part of the world's intelligent workers have become irreligious, or at least, uninterested in religion.

—Dorothy Sayers

When I asked Peter Drucker, then aged eighty-six, which of his twenty-six books he was proudest of, he responded, "The next one."

—Jim Collins

Perhaps no book in the modern era has more informed the way Christian professionals think about their careers than Bob Buford's 1994 book, *Halftime: Moving from Success to Significance*.[48] New editions sell upwards of 750,000 copies. The Halftime Institute, started by Buford in the aftermath of the book's success, trains thousands of church leaders and business laypeople, continues to advance the message of Buford and his book even five years after his passing. The basic tenet of Buford's book was that the first half of one's adult life is filled with "achieving and gaining, learning and earning,"[49] yet, as one makes "halftime adjustments," the second half of adult life can lead to greater fulfillment through self-realization, service, and deeper meaning.

Buford openly relates how his own economic success drove him to a midlife crisis,[50] but not one characterized by substance abuse or marital infidelity. Rather, Buford faced a "success panic"[51] when he realized that he still had decades to live yet had achieved all the success and material well-being he needed. This moment of "success panic" makes one vulnerable to depression, bad behavior, and, at bare minimum, a questioning of what life ought to entail going forward. The *Halftime* model of moving from success to significance is meant to neutralize that "success panic," even promising readers that the best years of your life lie in the second half of your adult years, as success will never completely fulfill you, but a "second-half mission" will.[52]

---

48 Bob Buford, *Halftime: Moving from Success to Significance*, Zondervan, originally published 1995 and updated several times since.
49 Ibid, p. 35 (2015 anniversary edition).
50 It is worth noting here that he also writes of the tragic loss of his young adult son, yet he makes clear to readers that this loss came as he was already in his "halftime" moment and was not the cause of it.
51 Ibid, p. 49.
52 Ibid, p. 12.

Agreeing Before We Disagree

Much of Buford's book seeks to promote an idea that I wrote this book to combat: the modern narrative that our adult lives consist of an arduous career for twenty to thirty years followed by a leisurely retirement for twenty to thirty years. Buford argues for a "second half" of life that is not merely "post-drudgery" but "significant"—leaving the self-serving monotony of career behind (as much as economically possible), yet finding avenues to apply and use one's skills, experience, passions, and resources for lasting impact.

That idea underlies the books, materials, and programs that have become a training manual for thousands of churches and non-profit organizations. Behind the *Halftime* message is a counter proposal for those men and women in the middle stage of their adult lives who either persist in long days and stressful (yet successful) careers, or else leave behind their careers for the "thirty-year vacation" vision of retirement I wrote about in the preceding chapter. Buford's work offers a "door number three," a lane whereby work, career, material aspiration, and the rat race can be repudiated (at least at "halftime"), and a second half of life that promises peace, fulfillment, and, again, significance.

I, too, find the notion of alleviating the drudgery of the first half of life with a thirty-year vacation highly problematic. Where I part ways with Buford is not in desiring a second half of life that is significant for people. We both want that. Rather, our disagreement is over the assertion (or implication) that the first half of life is drudgery, and that the significance of the second half of life is intrinsically separate from one's work and vocational calling.

There is much to appreciate about Buford's work. If the book were a general warning about midlife crises, it would be a good one. He is absolutely right that creativity does not have to wane with age and that the second half of our lives can and should be profoundly significant. I agree with much of the book, especially his advocacy for pursuing purpose, being deliberate, taking one's time, finding margin, being honest, having faith, listening and learning, and knowing what you believe.[53] These are things I promote in all stages of life, not starting at someone's "halfway" point.

This message of moving "from success to significance" is rooted in good intentions. I also believe Buford deserves credit for saying some of the right things: don't walk away from your work; don't mistake a change in jobs for the solution to everything that plagues you. He stresses that the path to significance isn't found through changing jobs, but rather through a change of heart.

He tells the story of a friend, a gifted executive offered the role of CEO at a large company where he believed he would have a real impact and earn a significant reward. Yet, after years of experience and achievement, this executive was considering going to seminary to execute what he thought would be better Kingdom work. Buford told him, point blank, to take the CEO job. Granted, he told his friend to turn the CEO job into Kingdom work by starting "an informal network of Bible studies for other CEOs," but he nevertheless gave the right advice about which job this individual should take.[54] I am not remotely opposed to CEO Bible studies; rather, it is the insinuation that the CEO job is not Kingdom work unless it leads to a Bible study network.

While there is much I admire about Buford, this book, and so many of its earnest adherents, I believe the book and its under-

---

53   Ibid, chapter 16.
54   Ibid, p. 102.

lying message has done great harm in the cause of proclaiming a holistic view of calling, work, and vocation.

False Dichotomies

The fatal flaw of the book is the false dichotomy underlying its entire message. I am appalled by the false binary he sets up between success and significance, the first half of one's life and the second, careerism and self-realization. I understand *why* these things are dichotomized, and how at times a careful distinction is perfectly warranted. But presenting these things as at odds leaves an incomplete and errant understanding of work and the meaning of life.

The subtitle of the book has become the battle cry of this evangelical movement—"moving from success to significance"— and embeds a thinking that is patently false. We agree that the sole pursuit of money and power can be idolatrous, but the notion that a productive career *necessarily* stands in opposition to a life of significance is simply untrue. Professional success can not only help fertilize certain extracurricular significance (as the adherents of the *Halftime* movement very much support); such success is very often intrinsically significant.

God cares about our business deals. He cares about inventions and innovations. The production of goods and services that meet the needs of humanity is not insignificant. So, why should all these successful *and* significant things be abandoned in a supposed move to the significant?

I admire Buford's desire for middle-aged adults to find peace and contentment, but the need of the hour is to present one's whole life as significant, not just life after the age of fifty. We should be defending and affirming success as a byproduct of a life well-lived, not a crass, self-serving pursuit that can only be atoned for by a second half of life filled with appropriate changes in mentality and activity. Our mentality and activity may very well look different at age thirty and age seventy, but that is not because the former is cursed by the worldliness of success and the latter rooted in significance. The binary assumption embedded in the entire *Halftime* approach is deeply problematic.

This binary is evident in the dozens of references to someone who has the gift of "making money," or "success," or "business," always in a semi-pejorative tone, but never with an acknowledgment or understanding that these all involve being good at activities that themselves entail service and productivity. To talk about one being "good at making money" without saying they are, for example, good at being an entrepreneur—i.e., good at producing goods and services—is either economic ignorance, or a willful omission of the most critical part of this entire subject.

To plead for a focus on that which is "productive, not profitable" is misguided. How does one profit without producing? It is hypocritical to like the fruit but hate the tree. If we want to talk about unpaid service, pure philanthropy and charity, and volunteerism: no problem. No one advocating for a robust defense of work and calling is going to argue that these acts of Christian love are wrong, and all will acknowledge acts of sacrifice, giving, service, and compassion as a vital part of a Christian life.[55] But it is rank pietism to suggest that our lives take on greater meaning when we shun vocational work. Christ's

---

55   It may be worth pointing out here that many who implicitly or explicitly proclaim acts of volunteer service or financial giving as inherently superior to vocational calling also seem to have a strong affinity for broadcasting such acts of "service." One can be forgiven for wondering if there is more than a little questionable motive in some who seek a spotlight and recognition for what is presented as virtuous and sacrificial. It seems that if there were a little more appreciation for understated acts of service and philanthropy versus what can seem like subtle (or not-so-subtle) vanity exercises, that case may be more credibly received.

Lordship covers all. This pietism is the inevitable consequence of the false dichotomy between success (work) and significance (other "superior" endeavors).

Buford, as a serious Christian, is clear that "significance comes when…businesspeople find a way to give themselves to God."[56] What is never explained in *Halftime* is why businesspeople cannot "give themselves to God" *as workers*. Only a sacred-secular dualism would find a problem with businesspeople giving themselves to God in their careers.

It occurs to me in studying the *Halftime* model that "success panic" is real, but it does not come because we need to make a different plan for the second half of life. It comes because too many people are being misled about the first half of their lives. If you aren't taught that your work is inherently valuable to God, and is an integral part of His Kingdom, it's no surprise that you'd panic upon finding yourself successful in a career you thought was existentially meaningless. A financial survival objective at least keeps your head in the game. But would we have an epidemic of midlife success panic if we taught the existential benefits of work to people in all stages of life? I think not.

The book's title and messaging use the sports analogy of halftime to evoke the image of a middle-aged person rethinking their life. Just as a sports team in need of new strategy may change their game plan in the locker room at halftime, Buford encourages Christian adults to rechannel their lives at "halftime," to move from working towards success to pursuing significance.

But the analogy fails in terms of advice to young adults. Instead of promoting a system of halftime adjustments, we should be encouraging people to play well in the first half. No coach

---

56   Ibid, p. 88.

would ever say, "My plan is to come out with a terrible strategy in the first half, then make adjustments at halftime and play well in the second half." *Halftime* essentially says that the first half of our lives is inevitably going to go poorly, and it's only in the second half that things will go well. I disagree. Why not get it right from the first-half kickoff? And by getting it right, I mean defining work as God's created plan for our lives.

First-Half Blues

Buford takes for granted that the first half of one's adult life is rooted in careerism. Not all midlife crises arrive because the first half of life is dedicated only to career success, creating a lack of fulfillment, with the remedy being a second half of real purpose. But let's examine the premise that the second half of our life (where we can find significance) is at odds with the first half (where our pursuits are merely pragmatic, transactional, and obligatory). Is there not room in that (false) binary to seek correction in the first half of life, rather than focusing only on the second?

Buford says the second half of your life is about slowing down, regaining control, setting limits, working with people you like, being missional, and so on. Why not take that approach to the first half of one's life as well? Why insist on this dichotomy? Even if the degree of margin and flexibility may be greater later in life, aren't these values equally valid for a younger person?

Buford would deny my claims about his view of a first half versus second half of life. But these are his words, not mine:

> Success in the first half is lonely because it is directed inward. It gains significance in the second half from the "pouring out" of ourselves, our gifts, our talents, our

resources. As you begin to hit your stride in the second half, pay attention to yourself.[57]

Casting the second half of one's life as the time for significance is rooted in the idea that financial freedom is earned in the first half. These "second-half" advocates explicitly claim to have achieved the success side—and then pretend they don't know how they did so. *"We did these 'success' things to get here, but now we want to tell you about the 'significant' things that matter."*

It is more than a little conflicted. Buford himself explains how at his "halftime" moment he was in a position to dedicate only 20 percent of his time to his company and 80 percent of his time to other nonprofit activities. He admits that he could still enjoy multiple homes, nice cars, and the same lifestyle (his words, not mine).[58] He goes on to say that not everyone can devote only 20 percent of their time to career, but he was "fortunate" in that respect. He then explicitly says:

> Don't let the fact you have to work for a living limit the grace God has in store for you during your second half [of life].[59]

I would humbly suggest that some people don't "have to" work "for a living" and that God's grace is not limited by any of these conditions or variables. Rather, depicting our work as a potential impediment to "what God has in store" for our lives is extremely unfortunate.

---

57   Ibid, p. 139.
58   Ibid, p. 55.
59   Ibid.

Kingdom Theology in a Box

Interestingly, the chief error in Buford's book is largely easy to disprove. It centers on one's "box," an imaginary storage place where one can only keep one thing. The question of what we put in our box is the main trope in *Halftime*. The problem, of course, is that it is not true that we can only put one thing in our box. In fact, each faithful Christian should have multiple things in their box, strengthened by a foundation of Christ. Our careers, families, church, and a wide array of other interests and passions all matter. They matter to us and to God.

The belief that only one thing can go in our "box of priorities" is fundamentally untrue. In fact, it's impossible. Once we say (as Buford rightly does) that the one thing in our box is God, we still have to define what that means to place God as the foundation of our ordered priorities. In so doing, we inevitably add more things to our box.

A Visit from an Old Enemy

When reading *Halftime*, one can clearly see that Buford had extraordinary instincts and insights for many things but lacked a theological framework for how to apply them. While he surely had no fondness for or familiarity with the Gnostic heresy itself, the *Halftime* concept is filled with latent Gnosticism.

He tells of a talented computer scientist who was told his "success to significance" meant leaving computer science and teaching Sunday school. Buford loudly criticizes this suggestion, saying the man could achieve significance by using his computer and business skills at the church instead. I applaud the improvement from recommending teaching to using this man's God-given skills in the church. But why couldn't he bring his computer and business skills *to the computer business*? This implied dualism pitting the sacred against the secular permeates *Halftime* thinking.

I heard a pastor say recently, "If you have time and money to put into work, you have time and money to put into ministry." Maybe some do have more time and money for additional avenues of Kingdom work. But that quote reveals a theology that pits vocation against Kingdom—our work against the church— and it is utterly wrong.

So much of the *Halftime* concept is captured in the question Buford repeatedly asks: *"Do you understand the difference between being called and being driven?"*

My answer: "We are called to be driven."

Holistic Purpose and Service, in All of Life

Let's live both halves of our life as driven servants of God: producing, growing, obeying, loving, and flourishing.

My criticism of the message that our lives are divided into a period of success and a period of significance is based in a belief about the Kingdom of God. I do not accept the premise that an elevated commitment to Kingdom means a diminished view of work. In fact, I believe a transactional, dualist view of work reflects a low view of Kingdom. I also recognize that not all adopting that viewpoint are aware they are doing so.

Yes, a significant number of people will spend their senior years with different priorities, schedules, and endeavors than those of their early adult years. But their significance did not begin when they cut the cord on their career, nor do they delay its onset if they keep working. God's Kingdom is larger than that. We have stages of life in terms of years and health and experiences, but our lives are not divided between success and significance in the eyes of God.

If anyone was in a position to view his own life as bifurcated between success and significance, it would be concentration camp survivor Viktor Frankl. The brilliant Viennese psychiatrist was a renowned academic, lecturer, and practitioner before he lost his father, mother, and wife to the Holocaust. After being imprisoned in the Bergen-Belsen concentration camp for three years and enduring unspeakable suffering, Frankl later said that he found comfort by imagining himself again one day lecturing to students, behind a podium.

After he was liberated, what did he spend four more decades of his life doing? Lecturing behind a podium.

A life of meaning, no doubt. A life of success. And a life of significance.

POUTING PULPITS
& PART-TIME
PASTORS

PROJECTION OVER PROCLAMATION

MANAGING DIRECTOR AT MORGAN STANLEY

*I would tell a lot more ministers to get out of ministry
than I would tell businessmen to get out of business.*

—*Anonymous CEO quoted in Laura Nash's book,*
Believers in Business[60]

I t may seem evident from the preceding chapters of this
book that I am not thrilled with the state of the Christian
church's opinions and teachings on work. I am struck by
the defensive tone churches take, presupposing that "too
much work" is the default sin of their congregation rather than
"not enough work." I guarantee that the latter outnumber the
former in every church I have ever observed or studied by a
wide margin. This is vitally important to get right because, as

---

60   Dr. Laura L. Nash, *Believers in Business,* Thomas Nelson Publishers,
      1994, p. 15.

we discussed in chapter 3, our very purpose as humans is to be productive cultivators—that is, workers.

I believe there are both well-meaning and less-well-intentioned reasons for the church's inadequacy in presenting a theology of work.

Inputs, Not Outcomes

First, the well-meaning. It is understandable that churches don't want to risk jumping from the frying pan into the fire. If their congregation includes husbands who ignore their families, they of course don't want to greenlight further family neglect. If they have a congregation filled with greedy idolaters, it makes sense that they want to decry materialism and greed.

The solution to the well-meaning fear that speaking the truth might encourage excess? Stop. Stop what? Stop being afraid of the whole counsel of God. Speak the truth. The soft-peddling and milquetoast preaching is not and cannot be effective. It is time to see truth and love as intertwined, not two separate ingredients to try and measure in appropriate ratios. Stir in all the truth and all the love, and then brace yourself for the outcomes of faithful courage. If you mean to preach against idolatry, preach against idolatry. If you mean to preach for a robust defense of work and productivity, do so. Where tensions must be held in balance, preach wisely and sagely. This doesn't have to be hard. Preach without fear of which constituency in the congregation is being offended. Instead, if it is true—preach it!

The courage to preach the truth can be found in recognizing that the responsibility of the minister is in the input (the fidelity of what is preached) and the outcome is best left in the hands of God (how inputs will be received and applied). This ought to be comforting to the minister: he is not responsible for what he cannot control. Nearly every pastor with whom I have discussed this has admitted to worrying that a pro-work message will be taken the wrong way. I am not an ordained minister, but I want to remain sympathetic to those who have an earnest and well-meaning concern here.

The issue of inputs versus outcomes is not unique to the pastorate. This principle is universal in a world where there is both a sovereign God and accountable humans. I credit the "inputs versus outcomes" distinction as a major part of my success in the wealth advisory business. Our profession deals with risk-taking in capital markets. Some people want to hear that their investment returns will be higher than they are likely to be; even more want to hear that their risk or fluctuation volatility will be less than it is likely to be. Everyone early in a career managing money or offering financial guidance runs into the conflict of telling the truth and losing a client versus embellishing results and securing the client. Those most likely to have a successful career are those who learn to focus on the "inputs"—the truth of what is presented, the tenacity that goes into portfolio planning and presentation—and to be totally content with the "outcomes," what the client or prospective client does with the information.[61]

This principle works the same way for a real estate agent attempting to secure a listing without exaggerating the likely sale price of a house or an investment banker needing to value a business without providing false guidance. Would a diet work if the nutritionist merely lied about the calories to tell the client what they wanted to hear? Would a doctor keep a patient happy by assuring them that unhealthy practices were acceptable?

---

61 I would be remiss if I did not give credit here to my advisory profession mentor, the great Nick Murray, who taught me early in my career not only this concept but this exact nomenclature.

This concept isn't complicated, but we freeze up when those tasked as prophets and priests are called to boldly preach Christian truths. Inputs are vitally important, and of course there is ample room for wisdom, tact, and care. But there is a point at which concern over how a message will be received must be replaced by acknowledgement of the "uncontrollable" nature of outcomes. A preacher must reserve his concern for the inputs.

Poor Excuses for Poor Theology

Though this is not the primary focus of this chapter, I am sure there are some less innocuous excuses for failing to proclaim a robust theology of work in our churches. Genuine theological ignorance should not be defended or excused, and yet is less sinister than other explanations.

Gnosticism keeps popping up in our discussion of modern error regarding work and vocation. Believing there is a difference between the significance of body and soul, the physical and material, and the earthly and the spiritual is a heresy that has bled into philosophy and ethics since the early church. A belief that the church is superior to other vocational callings is likely to come through in one's preaching. This dualism is not always intentional. I cannot tell you how many times I have heard someone say, "Your job matters to God—He wants you to work hard and do well," then conclude their thought with "so you can do more in ministry, church, and Kingdom." That is Gnosticism that sends a preacher off course.

Almost all errant preaching I have heard on this subject exhibited latent Gnosticism—unintentional, but not innocent. A common example is depicting a career as only valuable because of the material benefits it bestows (e.g., providing for one's family, tithing to the church, supporting other ministry projects). This is explicit utilitarianism (even if wrapped in Great Commission rationale), but it comes from implicit Gnosticism.

A Christian theology that values the incarnational truths of our religion—that God made man with a body and a soul and that his eternal destiny encompasses both—is the only antidote. We know that the Son of God was *fully man, and fully God.* We exist in both a material and a spiritual dimension, and we should celebrate this creational truth, not hide from it.

If we want to restore a cultural apologetic for Christianity, each minister of the gospel needs to ensure his presentation of work, calling, and vocation repudiates these three mistakes:

- Gnosticism (the material is subordinate to the spiritual)
- Dualism (the secular is distinct from the sacred)
- Pietism (intensity of personal feeling is superior to doctrinal truth)

Ensuring a message or argument is free of these three things would bring a new understanding of work, calling, and productivity. These errors are so embedded in our thinking, only a self-aware, concerted effort will enable us to shake them.

So much of the focus and critique in this book is specific to the church—a distinctive theological institution and concept—that I risk skipping over the conflict that exists in the messaging of work, career, calling, and financial resources. A relatively new cottage industry of "Christian philanthropy" has reached new heights over the last two decades. Institutions, funds, think tanks, and various not-for-profit organizations have emerged without a direct connection to a church or denomination whose primary focus is to advocate for Christian generosity and philanthropy.

I am not discouraging generosity or philanthropy. I am support-ive of any and all endeavors that faithfully equip and inform believers in the act of generosity. I work with a plethora of orga-nizations in this "cottage industry" and have known dozens, if not hundreds, of senior leaders and advocates in it. Many of them are faithful men and women of God who desire to see greater attention paid to Christian philanthropy. Some of the most heartfelt believers I know work in this space, so I do not offer this warning lightly.

The cottage industry of non-church organizations that advocate for Christian giving is not immune from theological naivete or grift, either. It is worth it to apply the criteria suggested above to these organizations, as well as to the church. They must make a conscious effort to repudiate Gnosticism, dualism, and pietism in their messaging, and they most certainly must avoid grift and self-dealing.

I wish I could say that I have little experience with these groups being torn apart by direct conflict. For several reasons, this space is more vulnerable to conflict and warrants greater diligence and scrutiny. It should be noted that messaging about careerism and vocational dominion conflict with the business models of many of these organizations.

I do not seek to make sweeping accusations, but rather empha-size that some organizations are more faithful than others in pur-suing a mission around the time, treasure, and careers of others that is faithful to creational theology and Biblical teaching.

Less Likely but Possible Cynicism

A more cynical read of the challenges in getting pastors to take the creational view of work I outline is that it works against the varied interests of the church itself. Churches serve their own self-interests when they preach that time should be less career-focused (and therefore more church-focused). The theory goes that pastors water down messages advocating for greater workplace dominion because it takes away from their volunteer base, donor base, and general support and enthusiasm level, at least on the margins.

I am skeptical that this is a primary or systemic problem, yet am sure that it happens at least sometimes. At the risk of taking attention off the more likely scenarios, conflicts of interest ought to be navigated carefully. Pastoral messages that can lead to concern here should be presented clearly and forcefully, and congregants ought not to listen to a minister with the worst possible interpretation in mind.

I have no choice but to write from my own perspective here, having spent over twenty-five years engaged in heavy dialogue on this subject with pastors and spiritual leaders of every theological and denominational stripe. I have rarely found their agenda to be getting their congregants to care about their careers less and the church's operations more. That level of transparent manipulation seems to be the exception, not the rule, and we can be happy that that is the case.

That said, theological errors of the preceding point, well-meaning intentions, and an additional possibility are all harmful in their own right.

Poor Work Ethic, Poor Focus, Poor Priorities?

The last possible reason why the church offers an inadequate theology of work comes from an entirely different category of conflicted motives. I am well aware that this may be met with outraged protests and shocked denial. Yet I am certain what I describe here is a real phenomenon, and that it needs to be said.

I write in the abstract so that the message may be clear without creating undue or unintended offense.

I believe one of the key reasons so many pastors fail to preach a Biblical and properly ordered view of work is that many pastors, themselves, suffer from a horrifically inadequate work ethic.

This would constitute a "not-so-well-meaning" reason—and I believe it is far more widespread than we want to believe.

One of the first oppositions I hear when I charitably and humbly make this suggestion is that such-and-such pastor works "all the time." If I polled one thousand people within the evangelical world at large, I'm sure that the vast majority would say that their pastor is overworked. But allow me to make a few points (without intending any dishonor) that might better shape our understanding:

1. I am specifically referring to the attitude towards work that most people have in their career—the understanding that sometimes boundaries are crossed, after-hours needs are real, and sometimes people are unduly critical. Anyone who wants to be coddled and insulated from any inconvenience or discomfort won't have a strong work ethic—be they a pastor or any other vocation. I think it fair to say that pastors often feel a greater entitlement to boundary insulation than the rest of us.

2. I am not counting in the tally of a pastor's work time his non-church work that may very well be "time spent" but is not "time spent ministering to his church." I don't care if a pastor has a blog or a podcast, and in fact these vehicles may very well be useful in ministering to a congregation via good

content, church growth, etc. But should extensive time in the comments section or messaging threads of social media count as pastoral work time? Are there other extracurricular efforts one can think of that fit this description? Pastors are susceptible to gray areas around their church work and non-church work and should be held accountable, in my opinion.

3. The time pastors spend in their own pulpits has plummeted in the last twenty-five years. I imagine there are situations where an associate pastor or guest preacher can be a very good thing, and perhaps it was excessive to expect a minister to preach around fifty Sundays per year. Add in the fact that many churches now have Saturday evening, Sunday evening, and/or multiple Sunday day services, and I understand the differences in evaluating preaching frequency. I am merely suggesting that it might be worth a reinvestigation of the ideal preaching expectations.

4. This one is by far the most important to me. Are we confusing the work a pastor does with their productivity in shepherding and ministering, because the church has bought into the poppycock that churches are really large organizations in need of executive and corporate management? In other words, is the pastor spending so much time on needless bureaucracy and avoidance behavior, on what can often be described as vanity projects, that the *actual work* of pastoring has become a side show? I think this is worth greater contemplation.

Caveats Galore

I know a lot of pastors work very hard and have sacrificed greatly for their congregations. I think that's the job (hard work and sacrifice), but I do not say any of this with a harsh or uncharitable disposition. I earnestly desire to offer pastors moral, spiritual, and emotional support. I absolutely believe in giving them the resources to do their jobs well, including appropriate support staff. I believe ministers should be paid well, encouraged, and have the boundaries needed to be devoted to their families.

Some of the most faithful and inspirational people I have ever met were pastors. Please do not interpret this as an anti-pastor chapter. If right now you are thinking, "How dare he say this about me!" (or "about my pastor"), all I can say is: I didn't. Those who feel it does not apply to them or their church need not take offense. I know so many diligent, sacrificial pastors that if you are one of them or yours is one of them, I am not remotely surprised.

But, dear reader, this chapter was written for a reason. Some people who have taken on the vocational calling of minister do have a poor work ethic. We have introduced corporate drivel about "visioning" and "strategy" into our churches. Time expectations and clarity of what is and is not "church work" have loosened. All I can say, as someone who loves the church, is that a declining work ethic from those in the pulpit will lead to a declining work ethic from those in the pews. Whether or not that negative feedback loop comes with a helping of pietistic theology, it does great damage to the Kingdom.

One additional caveat: I strive to be an open and transparent writer. I don't have anything to hide, and where I feel something in my own story may be useful, I am happy to share it. You may recall in chapter 1 my open confession that work was absolutely a diversion through some of the pain I suffered in losing my father early in my adult life. I am happy to admit that part of my axe to grind here is my disbelief at the difference in work ethic demonstrated by my father and by so many pastors today.

I doubt my dad would have taken well to the idea of a group of people coddling him, protecting him, and ensuring that he had the most comforts possible in his ministerial vocation. We will never know because, well, he didn't have that (to put it mildly). I know that the clichéd argument that "in my day we walked to school uphill in the snow for five miles" is not an effective way to keep people in suboptimal conditions forever. No one wants to hear ad nauseam how bad a prior generation had it, or at least not as a reason for keeping things bad today.

That is not exactly what I am doing. I am sure the limited resources at my dad's disposal and the different era and time do account for some of the delta between his work ethic and the output we so often see today. Yet beyond those variables, there is a fundamental difference in how he felt about his calling and what I see time and time again in contemporary pastors. I ask for your forgiveness of my stubbornness in holding on to the model of sacrifice and exertion he set over the coddled, part-time ministry I so often see today.

A More Famous Example

The apostle Paul represents the quintessential Biblical model of a ministerial work ethic. That he wrote, ministered, preached, and endlessly served the early Christian church is beyond dispute. Note how important it was to him that he model this work ethic and general spirit for others to see and follow.

For you yourselves know how you ought to follow our example, because we did not act in an undisciplined way among you, nor did we eat anyone's bread without paying for it, but with labor and hardship we *kept* working night and day so that we would not be a burden to any of you; not because we do not have the right to *this*, but in order to offer ourselves as a role model for you, so that you would follow our example. For even when we were with you, we used to give you this order: if anyone is not willing to work, then he is not to eat, either. For we hear that some among you are leading an undisciplined life, doing no work at all, but acting like busybodies. Now we command and exhort such persons in the Lord Jesus Christ to work peacefully and eat their own bread.

—II Thess. 3:7–12 (NASB)

Modeling Right Behavior

I earnestly want men and women of faith to be successful, productive, and fulfilled in their careers. I want that because that's how God created us to be, and He has equipped us with the tools we need to excel in our professional callings. When pastors model a mediocre work ethic, their example carries through to their congregation. Inversely, when a pastor has a servant-heart, is industrious, productive, and diligent, and does so without complaining or entitlement, he sets an excellent example for his congregation.

If we are to have a society of diligent and fulfilled workers marrying their passions to their skills, we need spiritual leaders who transcend theological error and embrace Biblical orthodoxy. We need leaders who see church as one aspect of Kingdom, but not the defining part of it. We need to cast off any pretense of conflict of interest in how these messages are delivered. And most importantly, we need a faithful modeling of workers "who need not be ashamed" (II Tim. 2:15 MEV).

"IMBALANCING"
ACT

OUR OBSESSION WITH WORK-LIFE BALANCE

FOUNDER AND MANAGING PARTNER AT THE BAHNSEN GROUP

Men's work is necessary as a foundation for their lives, but their families have an ultimate, irreducible emotional importance to them that their work cannot have. Nevertheless, among the paradoxes with which men live is that their work may demand most of their time and energy.

—Robert Stuart Weiss

Having spent over forty thousand words thus far pleading the case for a higher view of work, I am more than ready to make the case for a properly ordered view of those things in our lives that are "not work."

I anticipate that, at this point, I'll field criticism suggesting that my thesis fails to prioritize family, marriage, children, church, recreation, civics, and any number of other activities that fall outside the sphere of career, vocation, and work. I want to defend against those critiques before they are launched, and hopefully provide a proactive clarity on how the multiple priorities in our lives should be understood.

Calls for a more elevated view of family are neither rare nor troubling. In fact, if you recall chapter 1, I am one of the voices calling for that higher view. I argue that the benefits to civilization of the institution of family are so compelling that this is one of the rare opportunities for common ground in our highly polarized society. Granted, different camps have wildly different understandings of what a strong family structure looks like, but a basic regard for some aspect of family is more or less a given in polite society.

My summary of the lay of the land goes something like this:

<u>Humanistic culture when the economy is good:</u>

Low view of family in theory, high view of family in practice, low view of work in theory, high view of work in practice

<u>Humanistic culture when the economy is bad:</u>

High view of family in theory, low view of family in practice, high view of work in theory, low view of work in practice

<u>Within the church:</u>

High view of family in theory, high view of family in practice (sort of), low view of work in theory, lower view of work in practice

In secularized culture, two major anti-family forces predominate. One is more theoretical, elevating the needs of the individual above the idea of family bonds, and seeing family as limiting and even burdensome. Radical autonomy of self is celebrated even to the detriment of marriage and child-rearing. The second is more practical, bringing high divorce rates, single parenthood, and extended adolescence. There has been a growing divide between theory and practice on each end of the socioeconomic spectrum, yet each side possesses a certain approach to family that is trending downwards (one in theory, the other in practice).

The church has a clearer message to discern. For the most part, the externalities of a church experience reflect a high view of family and a low view of work. There are exceptions, of course, especially as one gets further from orthodoxy and historic Christianity. But on the whole, particularly within evangelical Protestantism and conservative Catholicism, the church's message about family is favorable.

This is a good thing, of course. But it does invite the question of how pro-family constituents (this author among them) reconcile their view of family with their view of work. The group that has been the target audience of most of this book includes those who hold a lower view of work—one that considers it merely transactional and fails to see its inherent meaning and purpose. This group is not the target of this chapter. Their unequivocal assertion is that one resolves the family-work discussion by making work a lower priority than everything else. Case closed, they believe. I hope I have made my position clear on that belief system.

There are, of course, many who would gladly say that they value both work and family. I would. They then suggest that the solution to this tension is something called "work-life balance." Well, I wouldn't. And I want to tell you why.

A Worrisome Cultural Obsession

At some point ten years ago or so, a client asked if I would offer a little career advice to their son. He was twenty-one years old, bright, about to graduate from a good college in a big city, and certainly employable. He had a good home life, high character, and was ambitious enough to want to come talk to his parents' investment advisor. His first question upon sitting down in my Manhattan office: "How solid is the work-life balance in the field of wealth management?"

Twenty-one years old, never had a real job in his life—"How solid is the work-life balance?" I never really bounced back in the rest of the talk.

I interviewed a candidate for an administrative position a few months after this meeting. I liked her a lot and was confident I would offer her a position, but I first needed to hear what questions she would have for me. She hadn't yet asked about compensation, benefits, vertical mobility, opportunities for professional development, or team culture. I was confident that our position in all of those categories was very strong, but until a candidate asks and you answer, you can't be certain that what you're offering will match what they're looking for. At the end of the interview, I said that I was prepared to make her an offer and asked what questions she had for me before I put one together. Her reply: "Yes, I just need to know what the work-life balance is going to be. I really don't want my life to be about an office job."

She was also in her twenties, a single college graduate without much experience, and seemingly couldn't care less about the compensation or career path of the position. She just wanted to know before we went any further what time she would get to the gym every day. You can probably imagine how that ended.

I have interviewed countless young people who, upon receiving a job offer, informed me that they couldn't start for a few months because they were first doing a three-month trip to Europe, or a two-month trip to South America, or a one-month trip to Timbuktu. When I explained that we couldn't wait that long to fill the position, they expressed dismay that I wanted to disrupt their personal time. I am sure plenty of you can relate to the career launch that a three-month trip to Europe was before you showed up for your first day of work.

To be fair, this type of incident is par for the course these days. These young people are victims of cultural programming, not the cause of it. This mentality has become systemic, something unrecognizable to my own Generation X and the baby boomer generation before us. As for the generations before them . . . well, let's just say that I shudder to think how things would go if a twenty-something asked my grandparents what their "work-life" balance was like in their twenties. You wouldn't want to see it either.

I am in no way criticizing the idea of someone doing anything outside of the office when they are in the early stage of their career. I am not criticizing someone having a social life, or time for exercise, or aspirations unrelated to their early-career job. I fully support dating, marriage, friends, travel, church, and whatever else accompanies building out a career. I worked a lot in my pre-marriage twenties—a *lot*—but I did have friends, I did take vacations, and I certainly went to church. The issue is not making an idol out of work, which I would oppose as much as I would making an idol out of *anything* (including one's friends, family, exercise routine, girlfriend, boyfriend, or kids).

Rather, the issue is the bizarre mentality that what we are after (and even *owed*) is some perfectly compartmentalized existence where the ideal allocation of our time is served up on a silver platter. This aim is foreign in the history of human experience, as is the audacity to even ask the question.

Your Life Is Not Closet Space

Our lives, priorities, passions, and responsibilities are not socks that all need to be rolled up and stuffed in one drawer of finite space. Neither are they different types of clothing that force decisions the way we must decide how many pairs of pants we want to keep in the closet versus shirts or coats or sweaters. The entire paradigm is wrong—from the vocabulary to the intent to the execution.

An unerring formula for how our time will be allocated to different responsibilities on any given day is as likely as any other crystal ball of life's mysteries and adventures. Parenting is full of unknowns. Marriage is as well. Oh, and so is your job. Placing artificial constraints on one of these variable aspects of our life because of a demand for "balance" is impractical, immature, entitled, and futile.

Different seasons of life present different realities. Some decades present different seasons than others, and each year differs from other years. We see this play out on a minute level every day— some days call for people to leave the office early for a kid's basketball game, and on other days we have to stay late at the office for a work project. That is the flexible and spontaneous nature of adult life, and post-adolescent impositions of a "work-life balance" clash with reality.

Disciplined people set habits, routines, and best practices, and then they allow for flexibility. That flexibility is an exercise in humility—the kind that recognizes that we are not God, and that "things happen." Work is not one outfit in our closet that we like, and neither are the relationships we hold dear. You can only wear one outfit from your closet at once, but ontologically we are always a husband or wife, always a parent or child, and always a worker not to be ashamed. These components of our life, ordained by God from creation as they are, do not get turned on or off like a light switch. It is crazy that we would try to do so.

I am more than willing to admit my occasional failures as a husband or father. I have most certainly erred at times in these roles, and I consider my wife and children saints for putting up with me (for a lot of reasons). But I do not believe one of those reasons is that I "work too hard." If someone were underperforming at work, their supervisor would not say to them, "You are just being too good a parent." We are only conditioned to believe that an overfocus in one area of life causes neglect in other areas with one thing: *work!*

"Work-life balance" is a poorly phrased euphemism for asking someone to work less, think about work less, or care about work less. No one has ever used that term in my earshot to describe someone who is too focused on kids, church, charity, or marriage. In recent decades, as people's time on the internet has often *obviously* harmed their performance at work, and often even their duties as a parent or spouse, even then we do not refer to this as a "work-life balance" issue.

Someone who regularly comes home from work and ignores their children, pulls out a non-urgent work project, and routinely works during a family dinner or activity is not struggling from a lack of "balance." They are being a rude, inconsiderate jerk. They are depriving their family of their time, love, and attention. Balance is not the problem; a failure to live up to basic human responsibilities is.

Dualism by Any Other Name

When we refer to a work-life balance, we are linguistically pitting two things against each other. We are presupposing that one is not a part of the other, and, in fact, that the two are to some degree at odds. Throughout this book, I have tried to dismantle the dualism that pits the sacred against the secular. I would suggest that an equally malignant form of dualism is this very notion of "work versus life." Our work is not set against our life, and our life is not in competition with our work. This binary is conceptually wrong because it is theologically errant.

In Christian circles, one hears a lot about a pyramid of priorities—God, family, and then our jobs. This structure is useful for exactly one purpose: to undermine vocational calling. Acting as though the elements of our life that God has called us to, that are important to Him, and that are instrumental in manifesting His Kingdom, are a la carte menu items that warrant some form of "1–10" ranking, is abhorrent. We have one primary loyalty because there is one God, and He will share His glory with nobody and nothing. Nothing is an acceptable counterfeit God—not our careers, our families, or our hobbies.

Once we accept that God is the sole target of our worship, obedience, and endeavor, the question is *how* we are to worship, obey, and honor Him. If you believe the answer is to faithfully do that which He has called you to—being a good spouse, a good parent, and a good worker—then there is never room to put these things in competition with Him. If we are first and foremost to love God, and loving God means obeying Him in the context of His redemptive work, then our marriages and careers are both part of that endeavor. They do not linger outside of our relationship with Him; they are an integral part of that relationship.

Someone does not say that they do not care about their diet because they want to stay laser-focused on their health. Their diet, nutrition, and exercise are all crucial contributors to their health. The modern attempt to pit things that God cares about against Him is a substitute for accepting His expectations for us. I do not desire a robust vision for family, work, and community as a *replacement* for Christian living; rather, these dimensions and paradigms *are the embodied context in which we serve God*, now.

Dualistic efforts to separate these things from one another are untenable and normatively wrong.

Old-School Solution

There is a paradigm that is clearly taught in the Bible, but it is not the idea of "work versus life." I alluded to it in chapter 3. Though it was codified in the Ten Commandments, it was established *through creation itself.* The need of the hour is not "work-life balance" but rather a "work/rest" paradigm. God gave us this perfect model in creation by working for six days and resting on the seventh. It was not merely illustrative—He normalized it as the model for us, too. And He did this because He loves us, not to punish us. He loves us enough not to want a life of sloth and waste for us. Instead, He calls us to higher productivity and purpose than what some infantilized view of work allows. And yet He also loves us enough to embed a need for rest in our very nature—after all, we are made in His image. The work/rest paradigm is a creational reality, and it exists outside of self-help books and modern attempts at self-realization. It transcends pop psychology and the seven habits of highly effective people. It requires wisdom in the particulars but exists on a foundation of creational norms.

God created us with a need for rest as part of our nature, reflecting His own model of creation. We forget this at our own peril. In fact, we begin inventing silly distractions like "work-life balance"—lacking any coherence or specificity—when we abandon God's own model of work and rest.

Discernments and Decisions

Human beings wrestle with many tensions in our adult lives. Sometimes we have to make difficult decisions if we love our families, take seriously our jobs, or want to be a faithful friend. Life contains a lot of trade-offs, and managing those trade-offs requires ongoing consideration and care. The notion of a "balance" whereby we perfectly schedule-block our lives is a myth that infantilizes young adults and totally distorts our understanding of the way the world works.

I am well aware that modern technology has made this issue more complex and challenging. Every dedicated worker faces the challenge of "turning off" in a world that doesn't really allow you, let alone require you, to do so. Various knobs exist that can be turned up and down around technology limits, access, and presence. It is absolutely serious enough to warrant deep contemplation of boundaries and limits. My view is not that serious commitment to work means being chained to one's inbox twenty-four hours per day or obsessing over work during family dinner.

What I am suggesting is that life provides seasonal realities that should be embraced, not shunned, and that wisdom is the need of the hour through our relationships, commitments, priorities, and discernments about trade-offs. A pietistic assertion about "work-life balance" minimizes the importance of work and encourages establishing a "balance" that's skewed against work to begin with.

A vigorous commitment to the work/rest paradigm is normative, creational, and rejuvenating. Our batteries need to be recharged. Some people need to do a little more to wear down their batteries; some need to take more seriously the blessing of the recharge that comes through rest.

In these discernments and decisions, we must never set up a false dichotomy of God versus the spheres of His own Kingdom, and we must never pit the myriad of special, meaningful, dignifying components of our lives against one another.

I need to end this chapter now. It is time to go for a walk with my wife.

CONCLUSION

CONTINUING TO RUN THE BAHNSEN GROUP, ADVOCATING FOR A FREE AND VIRTUOUS SOCIETY, AND FOCUSING ON FAITHFULNESS AND PRODUCTIVITY FOR AS MANY YEARS AS GOD GIVES HIM.

This is the true joy in life, the being used for a purpose recognized by yourself as a mighty one; the being a force of nature instead of a feverish selfish clod of ailments and grievances complaining that the world will not devote itself to making you happy.... I want to be thoroughly used up when I die, for the harder I work, the more I live. I rejoice in life for its own sake. Life is no 'brief candle' to me. It is sort of a splendid torch which I have a hold of for the moment, and I want to make it burn as brightly as possible before handing it over to future generations.

—George Bernard Shaw

Whenever we bring order out of chaos, whenever we draw out creative potential, whenever we elaborate and unfold creation beyond where it was when we found it, we are following God's pattern of creative cultural development.

—Timothy Keller

The Big Apple

I came down to a coffee shop right near the East River on First Avenue in New York City to write this conclusion. I have written this book in several different spots over a five-month period, but I find particular inspiration in New York City, not only because of what it has meant to my life and career, but because of the energy, drive, and aspiration that have always been the pulse of the city.

I am a Southern California-born-and-raised guy, but due to a career in finance, I have had significant connection to our nation's financial capital for nearly twenty-five years, with a particularly strong presence for the last fifteen years, and bicoastal residency for the last six years. Any Christian adult who lives in or visits New York is probably asked by other Christians around the country, "How do you stand it there?" People are rarely subtle in expressing either their disapproval or confusion that a suburban Christian guy like me could not only spend so much time in New York, but move my family here and, most shocking of all, really love it.

I used to think the motivator of this suburban or rural Christian aversion to New York City was ignorance or fear: the (mis)perception of a mostly unsaved, left-leaning city (you know, like *every single city* in the country). They see reports on right-wing TV about crime or traffic and adopt a nonspecific negative view. It's pretty harmless and extremely common.

But that is not what I now believe drives most Christian hostility to a place like New York City. As I have dug deeper into this subject and analyzed both my love for this city and the antipathy others have towards it, I am convinced that a central driver in the animosity evangelicals, in particular, feel towards New York City is its aforementioned energy, drive, and aspiration. Indeed, the city's "pulse" is repugnant to many Christians. Their knee-jerk aversion to the ambition, work, and ethos of a place like Manhattan has, in a lot of ways, been the subject of this book.

Of course, in this book I have sought to do a lot more than merely defend the climbers and dreamers of a place like New York City. I do not much care what various people think about any given city as much as I care about the real instincts, impulses, and preferences that constitute the foundation of this example. Fundamentally—and sadly—the reason so many American Christians feel the way they do about a high-productivity place like New York is rooted in a fondness for mediocrity. And I am more concerned with *that* than I am with what they think about this city. The symptom is not the problem—the sickness is.

But there is no reason to stay sick.

The Nature of Our Identity

I hope I provided some clarity in this book about the nature of our identity and where in it our work and productive endeavors fit. I believe the spiritualized language that many prefer to use often obfuscates some pretty basic and incontrovertible realities. The identity of a Christian is found in Christ; this does not alter the specific individual identity each human possesses. *All* Christian people find their identity in Christ; not all Christian people are married to a particular person or employed in a particular job. There are any number of specific "identifiers" that contribute to our unique identity, some carrying far more onto-logical meaning than others.

The notion that what we do in this life is totally separate from our identity is, of course, absurd. No one actually believes such a thing, but a lot of people feel extremely comfortable saying it, or flirting with the notion. The idea that what we achieve is not a part of our identity or how we ought to be remembered defies logical expectation. Perhaps there can be a problem with how these things are evaluated or expressed (for example, using financial compensation as an exclusive scoreboard), but the assertion that we are to view a highly talented and disciplined dancer no differently than a couch potato—which is to say without valuing what and how they work as part of their identity—is asinine.

Thankfully, we don't do this in any other category of life. No one claims that abusive husbands and loving husbands are the same, with no part of their identity as a husband tied to how they treat their wife. We know that our actions and behaviors matter. We pick pro athletes to admire based on their talent and achievements, not merely on how hard they try or how much they love the game. We distinguish between work bosses who were handed the role and those who genuinely lead.

We know that what people do matters, but we often choose to pretend it is just an abstraction. It is not. Activity and achievement are very much a part of our identity, and the only real question is how comfortable one is in saying so. Note that I did not say it's *only* career achievements that determine one's life or identity. The material prosperity that flows from one's career is not the core of one's identity. But *how* one works, whatever the outcome, is an important part of one's identity—one's passion, discipline, service, and purpose. We are judged by our faithfulness with what we are given, what we are called to, what resources we have, and what we invest into our respective callings.

Jobs and careers that carry more social prestige are not more meaningful to God than jobs or careers that are less esteemed. My assertions here are not snobbish, elitist, or pretentious. But they are meritocratic. Wisdom is better than no wisdom, and productivity better than no productivity. To those whom much is given, much is required.

The aim of this book is not to ask all Christians to become corner-office financiers or lawyers (truth be told, I would settle for a lot fewer lawyers!). The message of this book is not biased towards white-collar professions over blue-collar ones. It is not socioeconomic snobbery. Rather, the aim of this book is to reinforce the joy and purpose that comes from service. My goal has been to present that work as central to what we understand life to be.

Remembering the Human Person in the Work

I truly hope this book is an effective defense of *all* work being fundamental to who we are and what we were created to do.

This is as true for those who achieve much as it is for those in jobs they hate. Do I really believe that people should celebrate the act of cleaning toilets as much as I believe they should celebrate a high-paid, rewarding job as a corporate executive? Have I really given fair consideration to the drudgery, toil, and seeming futility many people struggle with in their jobs? I do not take that issue lightly. I continue to assert that every good endeavor matters, including tasks I wouldn't want to do but that meet the needs of humanity.

Let's not forget that there are millions of people who do not feel themselves beneath the jobs that are often described this way. There are many who love their work as cleaners, janitors, bus drivers, or other jobs sometimes deemed intrinsically inferior. I cannot judge from the outside—but I know work with service and purpose is always good. One person may enjoy being a waitress and desire the hospitality, service, and interaction of that job for years and years. Another may see it as a job to suffer through while they pour themselves into their dream of making it on Broadway. These things often comprise the sacrifice, toil, and effort we go through on our way to a different calling that better matches our passions and skills.

In chapter 1, I advocated for an "earned success" that comes from pairing our "passions to our skills" (borrowing from Arthur Brooks). Ours is a big, populous, and complicated world, and educations, backgrounds, trainings, and skills vary. I did not say that all people should develop the skills to do the same thing; I merely said that wherever work brings someone, they ought to devote their passion and skill to the endeavor and understand that the work they do meets human needs. Whether in a dream job or a "stepping-stone" position, the work is not meaningless, and the theological and practical principles of the book apply.

I am not arguing against lower-skill positions; rather I am arguing against a low view of career, ambition, and vocational calling. I do not believe the principles I present vary based on income or skill level. I am sympathetic to the different situations certain jobs present versus others, but it is my earnest hope that in all contexts readers have found a useful, meaningful way of understanding work economically, theologically, and ontologically.

I understand that we don't all get a trophy or do a curtain call when we properly close a sale or deliver a package, but I am confident that the principle holds. A job well done can prompt internal satisfaction, external honor from others, or sometimes both, all of which are meaningful. Earned success that comes from overcoming adversities, finding a solution to a challenge, and, in some dramatic cases, reaping the benefits of years of sacrifice and preparation towards a particular goal are the very moments out of the Garden of Eden that we were created for. It is the human person in the work—regardless of circumstance, hardship, or recognition—that is living the fullness of human identity, created to work, endeavor, and strive. Work is what we were created to do.

I've avoided the word "workaholic" as it is highly loaded and not often (ever) intended as a compliment. If the word is meant to indicate dysfunctional use of work to avoid healthy human relationships, then by all means count me as anti-workaholic. If it means one who needs the accolades of their boss, customers, and shareholders to provide their meaning in life, at the expense of a faithful, obedient relationship with God, let's all stand opposed.

But if what we mean when we use the term is a worker devoted to his or her craft, committed to converting potential into reality, then I suggest a full embrace of the concept. That said, it isn't easy to redefine a word that has been given a negative connotation in common parlance, and this is not a hill I would choose to die on.

Beyond the semantics, though, I would die on the hill of defending a vigorous and emphatic embrace of one's productive vocational endeavors. And I think *that* is what most people are *actually* opposing when they speak this way—not their heartfelt concern for someone who they fear is avoiding trauma, creating real harm, or trying to cope by staying late at the office. Devoted work as part of living into our full identity of Christ—that's the "workaholism" we should embrace. Our true concern should be for those suffering who are almost entirely removed from productive contribution to society or proud participants of identifiable sloth.

All the Clarity I Can Muster

What inspired this book is the implicit belief that care for vocational calling is inferior to other dimensions of the human experience. I believe that view to be errant economically, theologically, and ontologically. Our productive activities are not at odds with our relationships, hobbies, and other experiential dimensions. The pendulum has swung to a belief that all God-created spheres are good except one. As image bearers of Him, we should not tolerate that.

I believe in robust, committed, devout marriages. I treasure parents who make sacrifices for their children. I encourage volunteer work, philanthropy, and generosity. I see all of these things as core to the obedient Christian's life, and there isn't one word in this book that denigrates these concepts and practices.

The force and thrust of my book are against the attitude we've cultivated that makes hating on work, ambition, and drive extremely comfortable—almost as comfortable as announcing to the world how much you support generosity and charity. I want to suggest that constant public pronouncements of piety can easily fall into Phariseeism, whereas a faithful presentation of the unashamed worker is countercultural in an admirable way. Plenty of people are living out accomplished and fulfilling careers, but too few are willing to defend this calling.

This Moment in Time

American culture is permeated with a certain industrious DNA that is risk-taking, pioneering, and aspirational. It is not universal, and it never has been, but it spreads far and wide, thank God. It is also on the decline, just as the Protestant work ethic and great Catholic social thought around this subject are. We are increasingly adopting a view that "producers will produce and the rest will find something else that makes them happy."

And we are doing this at the same time we allegedly decry wealth and income inequality.

We face a crisis of inequality in a lot of ways, but there is nothing that exacerbates it more than the dehumanizing view that our "best and brightest" can produce while "the others" watch reality TV and play video games. It lacks creational theology. It lacks a reasoned view of human nature. It eschews metaphysics.

We live in a time when the message of this book will scratch several itches across society. The alienation epidemic in chapter 1, the stunted economic growth in chapter 2, and the theological errors that inspired chapters 3 through 10 all face a formidable foe if we advocate to elevate our view of work.

I do not know what will happen in our increasingly polarized and tribalistic culture. I do know that a declining view of work will only widen the social and economic divide that separates us. No one who prizes a pluralistic society should be content to enable sloth or adopt a "work is drudgery" worldview. No one should be willing to accelerate the alienation that comes from such purposelessness. We were created to produce, and that meaning is the meaning of life.

Full-Time

We should all wish we had more time with our families, more time in joyful recreation, more time in church fellowship, *and more time at the office*. We were called to a good life—a life of service, growth, love, and activity.

I ask that we understand work to be at the very heart of the meaning of life, and that we do our work full-time. If we get this right, we will be gratified at the healing we can bring to the ailments of both our souls and the soul of society.

I have quoted Dorothy Sayers several times in this book, a devout advocate for the intrinsic dignity of the human person. It is fitting to close this book with what I believe is her most important statement about the subject of work.

> *I asked that it should be looked upon, not as a necessary drudgery to be undergone for the purpose of making money, but as a way of life in which the nature of man should find its proper exercise and delight and so fulfill itself to the glory of God. That it should, in fact, be thought of as a creative activity undertaken for the love of the work itself; and that man, made in God's image, should make things, as God makes them, for the sake of doing well a thing that is well worth doing.*

—*Dorothy Sayers*

BONUS CHAPTER

SIX COMMON QUESTIONS ABOUT THE FULL-TIME MESSAGE

The response to the publication of *Full-Time: Work and the Meaning of Life* in February of 2024 surprised me in its positivity. Whether it was individuals responding to the book itself or the general response at speaking events or in media appearances, it was clear to me that there were a lot of people with whom the message resonated. This was, of course, encouraging, and it was interesting to see the diversity of positive response. Some felt that it was a novel message that ran counter to the way they had been trained to think about work (this demographic was an important target audience for me in writing the book). Others, though, expressed a longstanding agreement with this message, and appreciated that "someone else had finally said it." Perhaps most meaningfully, many people reached out to say that whether or not they knew the message already, they now felt motivated—challenged, even—to do their work better, to take their careers more seriously, and to adopt the practices necessary to flourish in their vocational callings. My objective in writing the book was never (merely) to change or influence a belief system (though it surely included that), but rather, to generate action. If a lot of people can now say they take their jobs more seriously but they do not do them any better, or feel any additional contentment from the work they do, the rhetorical or intellectual agreement is worthless. Faith without works is dead, someone once said. Well, the same can be said about this subject: assent without *work* is dead.

Yet the response to the book motivated me to write this bonus chapter. As the author, I sought to make the case for an elevated view of work, rooted in creational and ontological truths, the best I could. I anticipated certain objections to this book's message and proactively countered prevailing attitudes that I knew would oppose the view of work I wanted to promote (for example, the "Half-Time" framework). However, no author can anticipate all of the follow-up questions, challenges, headwinds, and trepidations that a book's thesis will generate. In the public appearances, audience Q&As, media interviews, podcast discussions, and more, that I have done since the book came out, a few questions and themes have presented themselves repeatedly. My aim in this chapter is to address the most common, material, and relevant of these questions.

These questions are all reasonable, fair, and understandable. I have never taken them as objections to the book's thesis, but rather needed points of clarification. My hope for this bonus chapter is that it deepens your appreciation of the book's message and provides a more robust framework for the *Full-Time* mentality. I doubt these six questions comprise all follow-up questions to my book, but I think they represent what is most on people's mind as they process the message.

And if these six questions require another bonus chapter following up on the seven answers, then we will know a full book sequel is in order!

**Is the person "stuck" in a "dead-end" job *really*
supposed to feel that work is the meaning of his life?**

In a lot of ways, I did address this subject in *Full-Time*, but it is
such an understandable response to the more provocative claims
I make about work, it warrants additional treatment. I anticipated that there would be a divide in readers' responses to the
book's emphasis on socio-economic prominence in one's work.
However, I think this question is about more than merely the
social status or economic opportunity of a given job.

First, there is a need to clarify the distinctions between "start-up"
jobs, "rank and file" jobs, and "dead-end" jobs. These are three
separate categories, but they can be conflated in a way that distorts proper perspective. A "start-up" job can be boring, labori-
ous, and frustrating, but the solution to that Genesis 3 drudgery
is the fact that it is—wait for it—a start-up job! It is consciously
and intentionally part of a timeline and thus cannot be fairly
called a "dead-end" job. In fact, "start-up" towards a "greater
outcome" is, by definition, not "dead-end." Now, certain "start-
ups" may fail—and certain career trajectories or paths or plans
may not materialize, but that is not the same thing as a "dead
end." I would argue that sometimes a start-up is the most meaningful work, attaching all the aspirations, hopes, and dreams of
the human spirit to something further out, even if that reach is
long. There may be truly unpleasant (but necessary) work early
in a career, but it is best described as the first inning of a nine-in-
ning game—again, the opposite of a "dead-end" job.

"Rank and file" is easy to delineate from "start-up" but harder
to distinguish from "dead end." Some may find a "rank and
file" job to be "dead end"—but it does not follow that all such
positions are dead end. I would suggest that a rank and file

job is one where the person who holds it has little autonomy in executing it; their role is determined by other managers or decision-makers and is likely easily replaced. In other words, if Bill stops taking pieces of plastic off the assembly line and dropping them in a box, Frank could take over easily. Bill's role can feel quite meaningless to Bill, knowing he had no input into the process's design, how it could be improved, or even why he is needed when Frank could replace him and no one would know the difference. This setup can feel impersonal and meaningless, inspiring expressions like "cog in the machine."

A couple of comments are in order before I move on to "dead end." These "rank and file" jobs have two components to them: the macro and the micro. At a macro level, the task is not meaningless or it would not be performed. If the production of some good or service weren't meeting a need, it wouldn't happen. By thinking through the macro functionality of the good or service being produced, workers should be able to recognize the benefit of that production. But that is of limited utility to a worker trying to evaluate the concepts I describe in my book, e.g., dignity, creative output, and productivity, if they feel that all *they* are doing is dropping a piece of plastic in a box. Let me be clear: assembly line/manufacturing jobs are hardly the only ones where a "rank and file" designation is appropriate. Far more middle managers are "rank and file" than they would like to admit. More opportunity exists to feel "rank and file" than is commonly recognized.

Let's start with the most important point: *no one is indispensable.* Bill may feel especially replaceable in the prior example, but he is not alone. Even highly creative and productive professionals are far more easily replaced than they tell themselves at night. This is not because the work or the worker's contributions are insignificant, but rather because the world is large and each of us is only a small part of it. Yes, a meaningful part, but a truly humble Christian person recognizes their own dispens-ability even as they appreciate being an image-bearer. This ten-sion should exist for all workers. But is one with a more clearly defined "rank and file" role really to view their work in the ele-vated manner I describe in *Full-Time*?

My theology of work involves two concepts that are pertinent to the *economics* (human action and calculation) of this question: (1) In the role a person plays in a given situation, their work matters; and (2) People are free and capable and rational, and may very well want to move beyond the "rank and file" (or, per-haps, move to a different "rank and file"—from one assembly line to another). What is not up for debate is that the rank and file worker is performing a function that matters, producing, and meeting a human need. That person may feel that their talents, skills, and aspirations may call for them to pursue something else—and they have decisions to make about the risks they are willing to take, the certifications they want to obtain, the doors they want to open. Contentment with their role is an option; performing the role while pursuing (either in theory or in prac-tice) something else are both legitimate options. But staying in the role and believing it to be meaningless is not. If one human is doing work and another human is benefitting from that work, they are inherently doing something of meaning and value.

"Dead-end" jobs where even the highest rung of the ladder feels unsatisfying and menial can be mentally and emotionally tiring, even depressing. I am very sympathetic to the view that this is part of the Genesis 3 struggle and curse. But let's return to that pivotal distinction: the curse is not working a job where one feels unchallenged or unstimulated, but rather believing that only tedious work is available, or that "dead-end" work must be performed to meet one's needs. The work is not the curse, but rather the box one feels trapped in.

What I would say with conviction, optimism, and sincerity is this: I envision a market economy in which "dead-end" jobs for one can be "satisfying" jobs for others—and where "dead-end" jobs can be temporary sources of support while an individual aims for a bigger target.

A "dead-end" job does not preclude a "side hustle" (as long as we are building a whole question and answer around jargon). For some, it may be stopping at Starbucks on the way home from a "dead-end" job, before spending an hour a night work-shopping plans for their next step. For others, it may be refusing to accept that they have no input into the creative process of a job, and instead recognizing that they do the work so well and for so long that eventually managers and owners will want their input on how to improve processes and structures. And yes, for some, it may be transforming how they think and talk about their job, replacing "dead end" with "service."

But where there is a worker, there is a person made to produce, in the image of God. And where there is work, there is activity designed to benefit another human. In this scenario, work can never be considered meaningless. Yes, it can be tedious. It can be temporary. It can be one part of a journey. But it cannot be unimportant.

Does the "Full-Time" message apply to homemakers?

This is by far the most frequent question that has been asked by largely Christian audiences since the book came out, and I regret not preemptively addressing it in *Full-Time*. The book was intentionally targeted at those working outside of the home in a compensatory context (i.e., those who had jobs or need jobs, and who are paid for them); the flaws in many people's approach to these vocational endeavors was the *raison d'etre* of the book. However, not only does the message of *Full-Time* apply to homemakers, I would argue that it applies *in spades*.

This question is complex and can potentially become a rabbit hole, or at least an unhelpful distraction, in exploring the subject at hand. My thesis is that work has profound meaning, and that we do great damage to ourselves, and the world around us, when we treat it as merely transactional. I have made the case for our work being a calling and core part of our identity, spiritually significant to our Creator, who tasked us with working in the world He created for our cultivation. I focused only on compensatory work, because the principal attitude I sought to transform was that of people who had jobs, were paid for them, and didn't view that work as significant. But though there is no W-2 or 1099 attached to this work, the work of the "homemaker"—someone focused on raising children, caring for the home, supporting a spouse, and other such functions—also falls under the scope of this book.

In fact, who produces more goods or services than a homemaker?

Far from being outside the message of *Full-Time*, homemaking is a God-ordained function that is creational, productive, sacrificial, service-oriented, and intrinsically valuable. It is both subjective and objective: the work of the homemaker matters to God because the subject of the work, the homemaker herself, matters to God, *and* it is done for the benefit of an external human object, i.e., the family being served by it. In fact, although homemaking most obviously serves the needs of the family, its effects are more extensive. Communities are served by the work of the homemaker, as family formation impacts neighborhoods, and, by extension, entire cities.

It was never the argument of *Full-Time* that only work with a paycheck confers dignity. Rather, it applies to all work that is productive (material), is economic (allocates resources towards the production of goods and services), and is service (someone benefits from it). If anyone believes this doesn't apply to homemakers, they didn't get that message from *Full-Time*, nor have they spent enough time observing the work of homemakers—work that is, truly, full-time.

What can employers do better to facilitate the message of "Full-Time"?

In *Full-Time*, I focused on employees, not employers, and that needs some correction. I made the case that workers ought to have energy for their work, passion rooted in the theological truth in what they do, and a belief that their daily endeavors confer the dignity that comes from being created in the image of God. But these principles don't just apply to employees; employers should have skin in the game, too. Indeed, if I am going to argue (as I do in chapter 7) that retirement is a misguided notion that often implies that the purpose of work is to stop having to do it, I must also call on employers to not contribute to this misguided mess.

Allow me to lay out four suggestions for how employers can better serve the cause of *Full-Time*:

1. **Create and cultivate a culture** in your company or place of work that is exciting, respectful, and honoring of the human person, and that conveys that you believe the work your employees do matters. In short, not only do employees need to work without shame, but employers also need to cultivate a culture that supports this. Reward hard work. Punish lazy workers. Use incentives. Drive a spirit of collaboration and positivity such that people never have to question if their work matters.

2. **Eliminate forced retirement ages.** Perhaps this will entail a shift in how you use the more senior members of your workforce. Consider mentorship programs, consultancies, or other ways in which wisdom and experience can be harnessed even as age and stage realities are addressed. Do not draw hard and fast lines that force people out, demeaning them and cheapening their lifetime of work, at age sixty or sixty-five. Do not act only in the face of the threat of ageism lawsuits. Foster an efficient system for honoring senior members of your workforce, not as charity to them, but to the betterment of the organization.

3. **Reduce bureaucracy.** Nothing contributes more to employees feeling their work is futile than wasteful, inefficient exercises. Some level of process is inevitable, and most companies have some degree of bureaucracy imposed upon them by the heavy

burden of governmental regulations. But where you have room to limit or improve bureaucracy, do so. Facilitate an environment where employees are producing goods and services and serving customers, not doing excessive paperwork, sitting in endless meetings, or dealing with inefficient chains of command. Tighten the ship, not merely to improve your own profits (though that, too), but to cultivate a better *full-time* experience for your people

4. **Treat your employees well.** This is Biblical in the most obvious of senses. It is also pragmatic, in that talent retention and continuity is a vital part of business success. Furthermore, it elevates the significance of work. Fair but generous compensation, a culture of encouragement, reasonable flexibility where warranted, and placing visible value on the best efforts of your employees—these are the basic things needed from today's employers. This is a very different ethos from that frequently found in modern workplaces, where employees are either treated like chattel or infantilized, where they are told they don't have to come to work, where pet care is treated as a sacred right, where snack bars and day cares are heralded as a sign that employees are valued. Employers fail to communicate that their workplace is (as the name indicates) a place of work, not a spa or recreation facility. That said, employees should still be treated with dignity, fairness, honesty, and respect. This false, but common, dichotomy is a true

reflection of the flaws of our age: we are forced to choose between an impersonal and almost abusive framework, and allowing employees to skateboard to the office juice bar. Reject those two options, and instead treat your employees well, but like adults.

Is "quiet quitting" sinful?

Quiet quitting is as sinful as any other explicit violation of a Biblical commandment. We are to do our work as "workers who need not be ashamed" (II Tim. 2:15). We are to work "heartily, as for the Lord, rather than men" (Col. 3:23). There is no room in the Christian conception of work for "bare minimal exertion." It is not something that could lead to sin, but rather, is inherently sinful itself.

Can one be "Full-Time" but in a non-compensated role, as a volunteer at a charity, for example?

One of the critiques of *Full-Time* to which I took the most exception was that I did not believe volunteerism or non-compensatory work was legitimate. I already addressed this when it comes to the role of homemakers. But I most certainly do not believe that work, whether it be homemaking or some other form of "unpaid" exertion, is illegitimate. Let's draw a few distinctions, though.

Collecting seashells is not work; it is a hobby. It does not produce goods or services, nor does it meet the needs of others. You may like it (please don't tell me if you do), but it is not work. If the asker of the question above is motivated by not wanting to do work at a job but rather wanting to collect seashells, I am aligned with John Piper: I believe they are wasting their life.

But volunteering at a charity is not collecting seashells. There are all sorts of unpaid endeavors that are creative, artistic, humanitarian, and philanthropic, *and* that are productive. Now, one problem I have with those who default to classifying this type of human endeavor as a sub-category for *work* is that they often do so without acknowledging economic reality. If someone is able to do volunteer work or artistic work without economic compensation, *it presupposes that they, or someone else, have already satisfied certain economic realities.* In other words, some paid production of goods and services had to be performed before any uncompensated production of goods and services could be done. I'd rather have this conversation with that economic reality acknowledged. With that stated, the idea that work must be compensated is untrue and was not stated in *Full-Time.* I believe those exceptional cases where one is devoted to production of goods and services that meet the needs of others in a context that is non-compensatory can still be meaningful, dignifying, and existentially significant.

I just want to distinguish that from a hobby.

What should someone do if they hate their job?

They have a few choices if they want to live a contented life of peace and joy even in the face of discontent with their job. Allow me to close out this bonus chapter with a few options if you find yourself in this situation:

Evaluate the reason you hate your job, and if it is legitimate, is fixable, and warrants further exploration. Do you hate it because you don't like a boss or coworker, or because the work itself isn't stimulating? A deeper dive into the specifics of why you hate it is in order. This may solve the problem on its own, with no further steps necessary.

Begin looking for a new job while still executing the job you are currently dissatisfied with to the best of your ability. Stay focused, diligent, and faithful in the job you want to exit, while taking steps necessary to find work where you will be more fulfilled.

Evaluate if the issue is the job and work, or if your unhappiness springs from your own attitude. Yes, it may very well be the work. The job may not align with your skills, talents, and interests. There may be something to fix. *But* you should carefully consider whether there is a "grass is greener" naivete at play, and that a new job won't fix your discontentment. If you determine what you need is actually a better attitude and approach to work (or life!), give that a shot. It may just change your life.

With the Full-Time mentality, we do not only live out obedient faithfulness to God's created design for our lives. We also experience the blessing of purpose and activity where abundant joy and meaning can be found. This remains my wish for all of you.

APPENDIX

THE WORK-FROM-HOME CRAZE AS PART OF THE ANTI-WORK MOVEMENT

A crazy thing happened well after I first developed a vision for this book. Out of the 2020 lockdowns born of political interference in the COVID pandemic, a movement of people "working from home" became increasingly popular. The lockdown revealed it was possible for many professions to work remotely, with cloud computing, video technology, and the like. Even after the spread had stopped and businesses reopened, many chose to stay homebound, and many employers were willing to accommodate them. As I write this in the summer of 2023, tens of millions of former office jobs are performed daily by people at home, in their sweatpants, with either very limited office presence or none at all.

Of course, a key phrase in the preceding paragraph is "many professions." No one has found a way yet for those in the food and beverage industry, for example, to wait on tables or clean the kitchen from their apartments. Factory line workers are not familiar with the term "hybrid." Construction workers do not get to use shovels or power tools from their backyard pool. But hey, a lot of white-collar jobs are now considered "workplace optional." Who says we aren't concerned with inequality in our country? I mean, what could be more unifying than telling half the country to "come and go as you please" while telling the other half to "grab your power tools and get to work!"

Of course, there are plenty of legitimate reasons someone may want or benefit from workplace flexibility. Some self-employed people and freelance workers without coworkers or a culture of collaboration to protect likely found home offices and Starbucks patios a useful venue for work long before COVID. Even in the post-COVID world that I so criticize, there are surely exceptions where flexibility or reduced need for in-office work make sense. I do not write this appendix for the exceptions to the rule, but rather for the rule itself.

Generally speaking, the "work from home" moment has nothing to do with "work-life balance" or "more time with kids" or even "reduced expenses at the office." The irony of these "hybrid" atrocities is that they *add to the expense structure* as companies have to pay a lease for thirty days per month even if the office is only being used for ten days, all while adding home office and technology expenditures. But the excuses for the "work from home" aspiration can all be reduced to one fundamental thing: low regard for the work itself.

We err substantially when we fail to see the origins of certain things. People working together in an office was part of spontaneous order that rationally and productively coalesced over a long period of time. It just made sense: people working together can collaborate, connect, and communicate in a way that furthers a business's mission. Efficiency is realized when people share ideas, debate points of strategy, and react to challenges in real time. The office fosters not only collaboration and culture within companies, but also a brand. Businesses that have thousands of people each working on a separate island, at varying degrees of digital connection, but without the chemistry and connectivity of daily physical presence, will not enjoy the same culture, collaboration, and brand as those who do. A virtual workplace is not an *actual* workplace.

Thankfully, businesses all over the country, both large and small, are abandoning the silliness of work-from-home coddling en masse. What sounded good to say in 2021 has come up against the cold, harsh reality of 2023. Employees are less accountable when working from home. People are less productive when they don't have clearly established work hours. And the attitude towards work is impacted by things as mundane as wardrobe choices and the little tics we develop in our work routines.

There was also a real lapse of regard for community during the work-from-home moment. The dry cleaners, bars, gyms, coffee shops, restaurants, and other amenities that make up the "work-from-work" infrastructure were left for dead, often classed as "nonessential." As our crisis of alienation grows increasingly severe, it seems outrageous that we would advocate for more twenty-seven-year-olds who live by themselves also to work by themselves, cut off from these points of contact in community life. Whether it be the social needs of the worker or the business needs of the immigrant-owned dry cleaner or mom-and-pop diner, the work-from-home moment suffered from severe myopia in failing to see the big picture of its impact and aftermath.

Fundamentally, there is something satisfying about shared success and shared challenge in a workplace setting. Celebrating victories and working through obstacles in physical proximity is an integral part of our professional endeavors. I am fully aware that each company can, and must, navigate the particulars of this individually, and that modern technology has expanded certain flexibilities beyond what may have existed in 1962 on Madison Avenue. But human nature has not changed, and the benefits of working together, seeing each other, and experiencing community and connectivity in person remains a valuable part of the creative and productive process. This isn't going to change, no matter how much easier and faster the cloud makes data storage and file sharing. Technology changes; human nature does not.

In closing, I want to point out two things that I never hear anyone address in the debate about working from home. First, the cost to young workers in the work-from-home craze is massive. They are being deprived of two things that every older, successful person had: mentorship and the opportunity to be seen. It is unforgivable that a fifty-year-old today is pushing to work from home with no one else around when that same fifty-year-old was once a twenty-five-year-old learning every day at the feet of a workplace veteran with more wisdom, experience, and chops than they had. Those of us who are older and more seasoned got to be that way because someone else often took us under their wing, mentored us, and encouraged us. They didn't teach us via Zoom. Depriving people of that mentorship is the defining legacy of the work-from-home craze.

The second piece is my pragmatic advice to younger workers. Let's say that you are good at what you do. Let's say that you work extra hard, have great ideas, bring additional value, and have a real contribution to make. My advice: Be in a place where someone will see it. Hiding in your bedroom with your great observations and contributions is self-sabotage. You will be more appreciated and receive more opportunities for advancement if those above you in the organization see your face and observe your value. This is an immutable law of nature.

I long ago stopped worrying about whether people express ire and disdain for my views here. I fully understand why some like working from home, and I am sure it provides more comfort, space, and flexibility for many. I am also sure it decreases accountability and diminishes some of the burdens of work (like getting dressed) for others. I mean no offense to anyone with my strongly held beliefs here. But my firm stance against the work-from-home moment is nothing more than my earnest stance for an elevated view of work, i.e., the subject of this book. I believe that continuing to buy into the idea that our work is a burden and we should do all we can to diminish it is fatal. No one ever defends work-from-home as being better for the work or for the people the work serves (you know, the customers of the business). We are always told it is just better for the worker to have this added flexibility. And again, the dynamic of each business is different and must implement particulars here that work best for it. I get that.

But I also know what is really behind the mentality of work-from-home, and it is not a call for more productivity, creativity, and innovation. Quite the opposite. The reality of human nature is on my side here. Businesses and workers that embrace the time-tested value of collaboration and daily presence will come out the winners. And indeed, it seems that each and every day, more businesses are acknowledging the wisdom of the past.

ACKNOWLEDGMENTS

I began this book with a dedication to my late father, Dr. Greg Bahnsen. From the earliest of childhood memories, I saw and knew a man who lived, loved, and modeled hard work. Though we had different callings, I could not have been successful in my chosen domain without the behavior, discipline, and commitment he demonstrated throughout my young life.

Yet I also have had a partner in life since a few years after I lost my dad who is every bit the wind beneath my wings that his childhood example has been for me. My beautiful wife, Joleen, has been my partner, best friend, and soulmate for over twenty-two years, and is every bit the angel most people assume she must be to be married to me. She has been unwavering in her support for me, and she has been an active partner in our business, a confidant, a strategist, a master in her craft of client and team experience, and a tireless worker in her own right. She managed our household while I was traveling the country, and she has accepted me, supported me, and in some cases tolerated me, even when it was not easy. She supported the writing of this book despite the sacrifice it required, and I cannot express how much she has meant to my life and career. Every unashamed worker should be so lucky as to have a helpmate like her.

My children, Mitchell, Sadie, and Graham, have not exactly gone through their childhoods without some trade-offs from a dad who worked as much as I did. They are the joy of my life, and I can only hope that one day they will remember me as a hard-working father who loved them unconditionally. Because I do.

As this manuscript was nearing its completion, one of the great Christian warriors of this generation, Rev. Tim Keller, was called home to his Lord. Pastor Keller is quoted heavily in this book, and his own book, *Every Good Endeavor*, remains one of the very few books in evangelicalism on the subject of work that is worth recommending to others. Far beyond that fine book, though, Keller's Kuyperian vision for juxtaposing the gospel and our careers was an inspiration. He will be remembered for so many things—I will remember him as a friend, mentor, and influence—but chief among his ministerial achievements was his passion for bringing the gospel to the Manhattan business marketplace. The fruits will be coming off of this tree for generations.

I am thankful for my brothers, Jonathan and Michael, as well as my Reno family, Brad, Vicki, Colin, Monica, Tate, Auden, and Lucy. And speaking of Monica, I am grateful that the finest editor in the land took on a mercy project like me. She remains a treasure in my life—my editor, cousin, and friend.

I am thankful to Andrew Sandlin, who has encouraged me in the writing of this book for many years.

I am thankful to Bill Prough at Edwards Movie Theater for hiring me when I was fifteen years old, just in advance of the *Die Hard 2* opening weekend. I am also thankful for Mike at Flying Fruit Fantasy and the lady on Teachers Avenue in Culverdale who let me paint her deck for $20 even though I had never painted anything before. I am sorry if she had to have it repainted. I have forgotten the names of some of the managers at Togo's and Sizzler, but I am thankful for them, too. It was never drudgery, I promise. And I am thankful to Scott Shuford, Bill Conine, Brandon Ebel, Michael Goldfader, Jeff Gilbert, Mark Zielinksi, and Michael Nahass, as well. From Diamante to Morgan Stanley, it was quite a journey. I wouldn't change a thing.

I have too many partners, employees, and colleagues at The Bahnsen Group to name them all (fifty-six at the time of this manuscript's submission). What I will say to the old guard, to our newer people, and to those who will be joining us in the future—this is a calling, not merely a job, and I am beyond blessed to work with each of you.

And to my many, many friends—too many to list them all and too horrifying were I to leave a name out—just know that I love you all and count myself blessed to have not only the faith, family, and work that sustains a man, but the friendships as well. You make my life richer. I hope I do yours, as well.

And finally, I thank the God who made me, saves me, and did for me what I could not do for myself. I have a telos each and every day in the calling He has given me, and I pray that my life will one day warrant those words I desire to hear more than anything else in the world: *"Well done, good and faithful servant."*

ABOUT THE AUTHOR

David L. Bahnsen is the founder, Managing Partner, and Chief Investment Officer of The Bahnsen Group, a private wealth management firm managing over $4.5 billion in client assets with offices in Newport Beach, New York City, Minneapolis, Nashville, Austin, and Bend, Oregon. The Bahnsen Group offers comprehensive private wealth services to multiple client segments, and David is regularly ranked among the top wealth advisors in the country by *Barron's*, *Forbes*, and the *Financial Times*.

David is the author of *Crisis of Responsibility: Our Cultural Addiction to Blame and How You Can Cure It*, *The Case for Dividend Growth: Investing in a Post-Crisis World*, and *There's No Free Lunch: 250 Economic Truths*.

David hosts a weekly podcast, *Capital Record*, a vigorous defense of capital markets and free enterprise. He also writes daily market commentary at www.thedctoday.com and weekly macro market perspective at www.dividendcafe.com. He is a regular guest at Fox Business, CNBC, Bloomberg, and Fox News, among other regional and national media outlets.

David and his wife of over twenty-two years, Joleen, split time between New York City and Newport Beach, though David finds the people in New York harder-working than they are in Newport Beach. They have three children, Mitchell, Sadie, and Graham.

David loves USC football, reading, and dining. His ultimate passions are his family and his work, as they should be.

For more information about The Bahnsen Group,
visit the website using the QR Code below.